THE OXFORD
HISTORY
OF
BRITAIN

VOLUME V

THE OXFORD
HISTORY OF BRITAIN

This five-volume series, edited by Kenneth O. Morgan, is the work of ten historians who are all distinguished authorities in their fields.

VOLUME I. ROMAN AND ANGLO-SAXON BRITAIN
PETER SALWAY, The Open University. *Roman Britain*
JOHN BLAIR, The Queen's College, Oxford. *The Anglo-Saxons*

VOLUME II. THE MIDDLE AGES
JOHN GILLINGHAM, London School of Economics and Political Science. *The Early Middle Ages*
RALPH A. GRIFFITHS, University College of Swansea. *The Later Middle Ages*

VOLUME III. THE TUDORS AND STUARTS
JOHN GUY, University of St Andrews. *The Tudor Age*
JOHN MORRILL, Selwyn College, Cambridge. *The Stuarts*

VOLUME IV. THE EIGHTEENTH CENTURY AND THE AGE OF INDUSTRY
PAUL LANGFORD, Lincoln College, Oxford. *The Eighteenth Century*
CHRISTOPHER HARVIE, University of Tübingen. *Revolution and the Rule of Law*

VOLUME V. THE MODERN AGE
H. C. G. MATTHEW, St Hugh's College, Oxford. *The Liberal Age*
KENNETH O. MORGAN, University College of Wales, Aberystwyth. *The Twentieth Century*

THE OXFORD HISTORY OF BRITAIN

EDITED BY
KENNETH O. MORGAN

VOLUME V
THE MODERN AGE
H. C. G. Matthew and Kenneth O. Morgan

Oxford   New York
OXFORD UNIVERSITY PRESS
1992

Oxford University Press, Walton Street, Oxford OX2 6DP

Oxford New York Toronto
Delhi Bombay Calcutta Madras Karachi
Petaling Jaya Singapore Hong Kong Tokyo
Nairobi Dar es Salaam Cape Town
Melbourne Auckland

and associated companies in
Berlin Ibadan

Oxford is a trade mark of Oxford University Press

The text of this edition first published 1984
in The Oxford Illustrated History of Britain
Revised text first published by Oxford University Press in five volumes 1992

British Library Cataloguing in Publication Data
Data available
ISBN 0–19–285267–1

Library of Congress Cataloging in Publication Data
The Oxford history of Britain / edited by Kenneth O. Morgan.
p.   cm.
Text based on: The Oxford illustrated history of Britain.
Includes bibliographical references.
Contents: v. 5. The Modern age / H. C. G. Matthew and Kenneth O. Morgan.
1. Great Britain—History.   I. Morgan, Kenneth O.   II. Oxford
illustrated history of Britain.
941—dc20   DA30.093 1992   92–1156
ISBN 0–19–285267–1

Printed in Great Britain by
Biddles Ltd.
Guildford and King's Lynn

CONTENTS

List of Maps   vii

1. THE LIBERAL AGE (1851–1914)   1
   H. C. G. Matthew

   Free Trade: an Industrial Economy Rampant   1
   A Shifting Population: Town and Country   12
   The Masses and the Classes: the Urban Worker   19
   Clerks and Commerce: the Lower Middle Class   25
   The Propertied Classes   27
   Pomp and Circumstance   29
   'A Great Change in Manners'   32
   'Villa Tories': the Conservative Resurgence   33
   Ireland, Scotland, Wales: Home Rule Frustrated   37
   Reluctant Imperialists?   42
   The *fin-de-siècle* Reaction: New Views of the State   48
   Old Liberalism, New Liberalism, Labourism and
       Tariff Reform   52
   Edwardian Years: a Crisis of the State Contained   56
   'Your English summer's done'   62

2. THE TWENTIETH CENTURY (1914–1987)   65
   Kenneth O. Morgan

   The First World War   65
   The Twenties   78
   The Thirties   91
   The Second World War   104
   The Post-War World   117
   From the Seventies to the Nineties   131

Further Reading   147 vi *Contents*

Chronology   153
Genealogy of Royal Lines   176
Prime Ministers 1851–1990   177

LIST OF MAPS

Urban population growth 1841–1911   15
The expansion of the British Empire 1815–1914   44–5
The retreat from Empire 1947–1980   124–5

1. *The Liberal Age*

(1851–1914)

___

H. C. G. MATTHEW

Free Trade: an Industrial Economy Rampant

THE Great Exhibition of 1851 celebrated the ascendancy of the United Kingdom in the market-place of the world, though many of the Coninental exhibits, especially those from the German states, gave British manufacturers pause when the high quality of their technology was examined. The Exhibition, sponsored by the court and organized by the aristocracy, reflected Britain's commitment to economic progress and hence to Liberalism. It touched an enthusiastic nerve in the popular mind. For many ordinary people, it was the first occasion for a visit to London, an exhausting but exhilarating long day-trip on one of the special trains which brought visitors from all over the country. The success of the Exhibition astonished contemporaries. Figures for attendance were published daily in the press; by the end, over six million tickets had been sold, and on one day over 109,000 persons visited the 'blazing arch of lucid glass', Joseph Paxton's Crystal Palace which housed the Exhibition in Hyde Park. Its substantial profits were later used to build the museums at South Kensington. The huge crowds were well behaved and openly monarchic. Members of the propertied classes congratulated themselves: the nervous, brittle atmosphere of the 1840s was giving way to the calmer tone of the 1850s, which by the 1860s had become positively self-confident. A street ballad sold at the Exhibition emphasized the

curious blend of artisan self-reliance, free-trade internationalism, and monarchic chauvinism which was to define the language of much of British public life for the rest of the century:

> O, surely England's greatest wealth,
> Is an honest working man. . . .
> It is a glorious sight to see
> So many thousands meet,
> Not heeding creed or country,
> Each other friendly greet.
> Like children of one mighty sire,
> May that sacred tie ne'er cease,
> May the blood stain'd sword of War give way
> To the Olive branch of Peace.
>
> But hark! the trumpets flourish,
> Victoria does approach,
> That she may long be spared to us
> Shall be our reigning toast.
> I trust each heart, it will respond,
> To what I now propose—
> Good will and plenty to her friends,
> And confusion to her foes.

The tone of ballads such as this explains the popularity of
Henry Temple, Lord Palmerston. When Lord Aberdeen's coalition government of 1852 foundered into war against Russia
in the Crimea (1854–6) and then disintegrated when the
ineptitude of the war effort was revealed, Palmerston emerged
from its ruins as Prime Minister. He held this post, leading the
Liberal coalition, with one short interruption until his death
in October 1865. Palmerston personified the bombastic self-
confidence of Britain as the only world power, and succeeded in
being simultaneously an aristocrat, a reformer, a free-trader, an
internationalist, and a chauvinist.

The society which the Great Exhibition of 1851 revealed was
given more statistical analysis in the Census of the same year.
Two facts captured the public imagination. For the first time,
more people in the mainland of the United Kingdom lived in

towns—albeit often quite small ones—than in the countryside: a dramatic contrast with the past and with any other economy. The free-trade movement accompanied rather than anticipated the commitment of the British economy to manufacturing, transport, and service industries with an urban base. That dream of the Liberal Tories of the 1820s, that the economy could be somehow held in balance between agriculture and industry, was forgotten with the free trade dawn. Agriculture remained easily the largest single industry and indeed increased its competence and output markedly in the 1850s and 1860s. But the growth of population was in the towns, and labourers left the land for the cities. When agriculture faced its crisis in the 1870s with the opening of the North American prairies, there were relatively few left to defend it. The 'Revolt of the Field' in the 1870s was a motley affair as out-of-work labourers struggled to organize themselves as wages fell and magistrates and farmers brought in the troops to harvest the crops. By the 1850s, British—and especially northern and midland England, South Wales, and southern Scotland—was thus, through the working of Adam Smith's 'invisible hand' of world trade rather than by any conscious political decision, committed to a ride on the roller-coaster of international capitalism, a ride where the travellers could not see beyond the rise or dip ahead of them: no one had been there before. An urban nation had no precedent: perhaps that was why the British dwelt so tenaciously on rural images and traditions.

The other statistic of the 1851 Census that caught the attention of contemporaries was its revelations about religion. It was the only Census ever to attempt to assess English religious attendance, or the lack of it. There were difficulties about the statistics, but the main emphasis was indisputable and surprising: England and Wales were only party church-going, and Anglicans were in only a bare majority of those who attended. Of a total population of 17,927,609, the church-goers were:

Church of England	5,292,551
Roman Catholics	383,630
Protestant Dissenters	4,536,265

Of potential church-goers, over five and a quarter million stayed at home. The Census was a triumph for non-Anglicans. Their claim to greater political representation and attention was now backed by that most potent of all mid-Victorian weapons, so approved of by Mr Gradgrind, Charles Dickens's Lancastrian manufacturer: 'a fact'.

England in the 1850s was thus increasingly urban, perhaps increasingly secular, certainly increasingly non-Anglican in tone. Mid-Victorian politics reflected these tendencies, all of which pointed towards Liberalism.

Between 1847 and 1868, the Tories (the rump of the party left as protectionists after the 1846 split) lost six general elections running (1847, 1852, 1857, 1859, 1865, 1868). It is clear that the Tories lost these elections; it is less easy to say who won them. Majority governments relied on support from four main groups: the Whigs, the radicals, the Liberals and the Peelites (the followers of Sir Robert Peel in 1846). This support was always liable to disintegration. The classic mid-Victorian political pattern was as follows: a coalition government was made up of all or most of the above groups, compromising and bargaining until they could agree no more and a point of breakdown was reached: the government would go out of office without dissolving Parliament; the Tories would then form a minority government, during which the non-Tory groups would resolve their differences, defeat the Tories, force a dissolution, win the general election, and resume power. This overall pattern explains the minority Tory (Derby/Disraeli) ministries of 1852, 1958–9, and 1866–8.

The political system between 1846 and 1868 thus excluded the Tories from power, while allowing them occasional periods of minority office. During the same period, the majority coalition first formed by Lord Aberdeen in 1852 gradually fused itself into 'the liberal party', though even when it became regularly referred to by that name in the 1860s it remained fissiparous and liable to disintegration. At the executive level, the Whigs, the Peelites, and Lord Palmerston predominated. To a considerable extent they ruled on sufferance. That great surge of middle-class political awareness exemplified in the Anti-Corn Law League in the 1840s had made it clear to politicians that the old political structure could be maintained only if it came to terms with middle-class expectations. The series of great budgets introduced by the Peelite Chancellor of the Exchequer, William Ewart Gladstone, in the years 1853–5 and 1859–65 went far towards meeting these expectations fiscally. The manufacturing classes wanted free trade: Gladstone saw that they got it.

'Free trade' of course meant much more than simply the abolition of protective tariffs. 'Free trade' or *laissez-faire* were shorthand terms exemplifying a whole philosophy of political, social, and economic organization. John Stuart Mill's *Principles of Political Economy*, first published in 1848, the handbook of mid-Victorian liberalism, put the point in a nutshell: '*Laisser-faire*, in short, should be the general practice: every departure from it, unless required by some great good, is a certain evil.' The presumption was that the State should stand aside. The division which Mill and others made between 'the State' on the one hand and society on the other was based on the assumption that the individual could and should stand alone. Individualism, self-respect, self-reliance, and the organization of voluntary and co-operative societies, these were the keynotes of mid-Victorian liberalism. Thus the economy should be self-regulating, and the individual whether consumer or producer, holding his copy of Samuel Smiles's *Self-Help* (1859), should be free to make what way he could in it.

This view of individualism gained from the widely popular writings of the social evolutionists. Charles Darwin's *On The Origin of Species* (1859) was not a bolt from the blue: it fitted naturally into, as well as transcending, a corpus of writing on evolution. The concept of evolution, and consequently of 'progress', whether on the individual, national, or global level, came to permeate every aspect of Victorian life and thought. Because evolution was determined by laws of science (a view usually described as 'positivism'), man's duty was to discover and obey such laws, not meddle with them. Hence most positivists (such as Walter Bagehot, editor of the influential weekly *Economist*, and Herbert Spencer, author of many works on sociology) were strong *laissez-faire* supporters.

If the individual was to make his way productively, he or she must be prepared and equipped with knowledge: the availability of knowledge and the freedom to comment on it was thus central to a liberal society. Moral choices must be informed choices: self-awareness and self-development in the context of human sympathy were the themes of the novels of George Eliot (Mary Ann Evans) and her own life was a testimony to the trials as well as the liberation of the free spirit in mid-Victorian society.

The abolition in 1855 and 1861 of the 'Taxes on Knowledge' (the stamp duties on newspapers, and the customs and excise duties on paper) epitomized the sort of liberal legislation which was particularly prized. The repeal of these taxes made possible the phenomenon which was both the epitome and the guarantor of liberal Britain—the liberal metropolitan and provincial press. The 1850s and 1860s saw a spectacular expansion of daily and Sunday newspapers, especially in the provinces, overwhelmingly liberal in politics and in general outlook. By 1863, there were over 1,000 newspapers in Britain, the vast majority of very recent foundation. For example, in Yorkshire in 1867, 66 of the 86 local newspapers had been founded since 1853. In London, the *Daily Telegraph*, re-founded in 1855 as a penny daily and as the flagship of the liberal press, had a circulation of almost 200,000 in 1871, far outstripping *The Times*. The new provincial press took its tone from the *Telegraph*, and that tone was unabashedly and enthusiastically progressive. A typical

example is this leader commenting on Gladstone's tour of the
Newcastle shipyards in 1862:

When we pull a political pansy for Lord Derby [the Tory leader], and
tell him 'that's for remembrance', it is because the violent fallacies and
frenzies of Protection are not to be forgotten simply because they are
forgiven . . . With ten years' honour upon her green laurels, and the
French treaty [of free trade signed in 1860] in her hand—the emblem
of future conquests—we have enshrined Free Trade at last in a
permanent seat.

By the 1860s, free trade—in its specific sense of an absence of
protective tariffs—had become a central orthodoxy of British
politics, almost as entrenched as the Protestant succession. The
triumph of the classical political economists was complete, in
the sense that the cardinal tenet of their faith was established as
a political principle so widely accepted that only a deliberately
perverse or self-confessedly unreconstructed politician would
deny it. Front-bench Tory politicians quickly took the view that
if their party was again to become a majority party, they must
accept that protection was 'not only dead but damned', as
Disraeli said. Tory budgets became as impeccably free-trading
as Liberal ones.

Outside the area of fiscal policy, there was less agreement
about how far 'free trade' should go. Pressure groups within
the Liberal movement in the 1850s and 1860s promoted a large
range of 'negative' free-trade measures: the abolition of established Churches, the abolition of compulsory church rates, the
abolition of religious tests for entry into Oxford and Cambridge and public offices, the removal of restrictions upon the
transfer or use of land, the end of a civil service based on
patronage. In addition to these, there was in the 1860s a general
movement in the constituencies for further parliamentary
reform—a demand welcomed by many but not all of the Liberal
MPs. The Liberal Party legislating on such matters was not
really a 'party' in the modern sense of the word. It was rather a
loose coalition of complex, interlocking allegiances, the most

basic of which was its commitment to a free-trading economy. Within the coalition nestled many reforming interests, especially of a religious sort. A great religious revival in the 1860s added to the number of religious activists within the Liberal Party, and to the enthusiasm with which they both aired their opinions and worked for the party's success. Roman Catholics, nonconformists, and even secularists found voices within this broadly-based movement for progress—the voices were given a common accent by their hostility to Anglicanism and the established Church. Non-Anglicanism was, throughout the century, perhaps the most important social reason for voting Liberal. Paradoxically, however, the leadership of the coalition was uniformly Anglican, though of a moderate and reforming kind. There was, therefore, considerable dispute between the leadership of the coalition and its more militant supporters about the speed of reform. On the whole, the leadership—Palmerston, Lord John Russell, Gladstone—wanted moderate reform which would strengthen the Anglican Church overall, while the radical rank and file wanted step-by-step reform which would lead to the eventual disestablishment of the Anglican Church. Both groups could thus agree on limited measures such as the abolition of compulsory church rates while disagreeing on the ultimate ends of their policies. The crowning success of this sort of approach to politics was the disestablishment of the Anglican Church in Ireland in 1869.

The participation of the articulate members of the working classes within the Liberal Party, especially at the constituency level, was of great importance. In the 1830s and early 1840s, the six points of the Chartists had constituted a demand which, in terms of the politics of the day, could not be incorporated by the classes holding political power. By the late 1850s, radical movement for constitutional reform, often led by ex-Chartists, demanded only changes in the franchise, and of these enfranchisement of the male head of each household at most ('household suffrage'). It was not difficult for political leaders in both parties, but especially in the Liberal Party, to come to terms with such requests. They also had their own reasons for wanting to change the system. Some Tories wanted to change it because their experience from 1847 onwards showed that they could not win a general election within the existing system. Some Liberals, including Gladstone and Lord John Russell, wanted to make marginal extensions to the franchise so as to include more liberal artisans, sturdy individualists who would support the Liberal's programme of retrenchment and reform. Some radicals, such as John Bright, wanted a 'household suffrage' to give a more full-blooded basis to Liberalism, though even they were quick to point out that they did not want votes given to what was known as 'the residuum' (that is, paupers, the unemployed, the 'thriftless', men with no property at all). Some Liberals such as Robert Lowe, radical enough on ordinary legislation, distrusted any change leading to 'democracy' as they believed the 'intelligent class' would be swamped by it. Some Tories such as the future Lord Salisbury feared a household suffrage would lead to an attack on property through increased direct taxes such as the income tax. Some Whigs saw no reason to change a system which always returned non-Tory Parliaments.

Palmerston reflected the views of this last group, and won a great election victory in 1865 without a pledge to franchise reform. He died that autumn. Russell, his successor as Prime Minister, brought in with Gladstone in 1866 a very moderate reform bill dealing mainly with towns, on which their ministry broke up, some of their party withdrawing support because the bill did too much, others because it did too little. The third of the Derby/Disraeli minority Tory administrations then brought in its own bill for the towns, thus selling the pass of the anti-reformers' position. Reform of some sort became certain: the Liberals had begun their customary regrouping when Disraeli unexpectedly announced his acceptance of a household suffrage amendment: the bill then passed, in a form a great deal more dramatic and sweeping than the Russell–Gladstone bill of the previous year. The franchise system of 1832 was ended: the parameters of urban politics until 1918 were established (similar voting privileges were granted to men in the counties in 1884–5). In an extremely confused situation in 1868, the Liberals seemed to reconfirm their 1865 election position as the dominant party by winning the general election with the huge majority of 112. In fact, the 1867 Reform Act had changed the rules of the political game in such a way that a majority Tory government again became possible—but it was to be a Tory government under Disraeli in 1874 which made no serious attempt to reverse any of the main Liberal achievements of the previous thirty years, certainly not the centre-piece of free trade.

The early years of Gladstone's first government (1868–74) were the culmination of these reforming pressures: by 1874 many of the demands of mid-century Liberalism were fulfilled. In addition to disestablishing the Irish Church, the Liberals in the 1860s and early 1870s had abolished compulsory church rates, the 'taxes on knowledge', religious tests for Oxford and Cambridge, and the purchase of commissions in the army; they had legislated on Irish land, and on education for England and Scotland; they had opened the civil service to entrance by competition and they had made capitalism relatively safe for the investor by introducing limited liability—all this in addition to their preoccupation with free trade finance, proper government accounting, minimum budgets, and retrenchment.

Though there was the usual tug and tussle of political bargaining, this great reforming surge had not been seriously opposed. Even the establishment of the Anglican Church—whose defence *in toto* had been a central rallying point of Toryism in the first half of the century—had been ended in part clearly and efficiently: what had in the 1830s been merely a radical dream had by the 1870s become reality, and almost without apparent struggle. The Tories' ultimate card, the un-elected House of Lords, had been played in only a limited way—to delay repeal of the paper duties, to delay church rate repeal, the ballot, and the abolition of religious tests at the universities. The propertied and labouring classes had collaborated in a great clearing of the decks of the Liberal ship of state.

The advent of 'free trade' as the prevailing ethos coincided with an economic boom, lasting from the early 1850s to the early 1870s. Contemporaries saw the first as causing the second; economic historians have been more sceptical. The removal of tariff barriers probably had only a marginal impact on the British economy, but the ascendancy of 'free trade', in its larger sense of a national commitment to economic progress, was closely related to an entrepreneurial enthusiasm which all classes seem to have shared. The mid-century boom was not, in percentage terms, very spectacular, and it was linked to a mild inflation. But it was none the less extremely important, for it seemed to show that the 'condition of England' question which had been so much a preoccupation of the 1820–50 period could be solved—was being solved—by market forces working within the existing social and political structure. Even the distress caused by the 'cotton famine' of the 1860s in Lancashire—when the cotton mills were cut off by the American Civil War from their traditional source of raw material, the plantations in the Southern States—produced little prolonged political reaction, and the propertied classes congratulated themselves that local initiative and voluntary subscriptions had seemed to be sufficient to allow the Westminster government to avoid accepting any direct responsibility for the sufferings of the Lancastrian work-force (though in fact a government loan scheme had also been important).

Compared with any other country, the British economy in the period 1850–70 was extraordinary in its complexity and in the range of its products and activities. It was strong in the basic raw materials of an early industrial economy—coal and iron—and it increased its world ascendancy in these two commodities as Continental countries imported British coal and iron to supply the basic materials for their own industrialization. An energetic manufacturing sector pressed forward with a huge range of items, from ships and steam engines through textiles to the enormous variety of small manufactured goods which adorned Victorian houses and, by their export in British ships, 'Victorianized' the whole trading world. This intense industrial activity rested on a sound currency and on a banking system which, though it had its failures, was comparatively stable and was, especially from the 1870s, gaining an increasingly important role in the economy.

A Shifting Population: Town and Country

This surge of economic progress produced a nation and an economy whose preoccupations were by 1870 largely industrial and urban. The growth of towns, which some had thought in 1851 could hardly be continued, intensified. By 1901, only one-fifth of the population of England and Wales lived in what may be called 'rural areas'; that is, 80 per cent of the population was urbanized, a far greater proportion than in any European country, and one which remained little changed until the 1970s. By 1901, there were seventy-four towns with over 50,000 inhabitants and London, 'the metropolis' as Victorians called it, grew from 2.3 million in 1851 to 4.5 million in 1911 (or 7.3 million if we include all its suburbs). The most rapid growth was not in the already established 'industrial revolution' cities, such as Liverpool and Manchester, but in the clusters of towns around the industrial heartland, towns such as Salford. These areas of urban sprawl went to make up what Patrick Geddes, the late-Victorian theorist of town planning, called 'conurbations', that is large areas of industrial and urban land in which several cities merge to form what is really a single non-rural unit. By 1911, Britain had seven such areas, at a time when no European country had more than two. These were: Greater London (7.3 million), south-east Lancashire (2.1 million), the West Midlands (1.6 million), West Yorkshire (1.5 million), Merseyside (1.2 million), Tyneside (0.8 million), and central Clydeside (about 1.5 million)—all this in a nation with a population of only 40 million on the mainland in 1911. Some towns, such as the iron and steel town of Middlesbrough, grew from virtually nothing to a population of 120,000 in half a century. Most of these conurbations contained a significant Irish community, and their politics consequently tended to be more 'orange and green' than elsewhere. At the end of the century London and Leeds also absorbed large Jewish communities, the victims of an Eastern European 'rural depopulation' as ferocious as the Irish famine.

Urban growth at this sort of pace was, of course, to be a common phenomenon in underdeveloped countries in the twentieth century, but in the nineteenth it had no precedent. It is not easy to generalize about these towns. Styles and standards of architecture varied enormously, from the indestructible stone tenements of Glasgow, through the 'back-to-back, two-up, two-down' little houses in the mining towns, often built of poor-quality brick, to the decorous suburbs of the lower and upper middle classes. A common feature of this housing was that it was almost all leased or rented—owner-occupiers were rare, though becoming more common by the end of the century. Some towns were well planned by civically-minded local councils, with parks, libraries, concert halls, and baths; others were left to the mercy of the speculative builder.

These growing towns were dominated by the railways, which created for the first time a nationally integrated economy. They transformed the centres of towns by the space which their stations and marshalling yards took up, they made it possible for better-off people to live away from the town centre by providing cheap transport from the suburbs, and they covered everything with soot. Filth and noise characterized Victorian cities—filth from the trains, the chimneys of factories and houses, and the horses, noise from the carts and carriages and horses on the cobblestones. When motor transport began to replace horses in the early twentieth century, everyone noticed how relatively quiet and clean town centres became. But noise, filth, and bad housing are relative to what people are accustomed to: it was only slowly that the demand for improvement in urban life became a powerful one. For many Victorians, production was its own justification, a view well expressed by Florence, Lady Bell, in her book *At The Works*, a classic study of a classic industrial town, Middlesbrough, a town given over to one pursuit and one only, the making of iron:

In default of a romantic past, of a stately tradition, the fact of this swift gigantic growth has given to Middlesbrough a romance and dignity of another kind, the dignity of power, of being able to stand erect by its sheer strength on no historical foundation, unsupported by the pedestals of Time ... And although it may not have the charm and beauty of antiquity, no manufacturing town ... can fail to have an interest and picturesqueness all its own ... Tall chimneys, great uncouth shapes of kilns and furnaces that appear through the smoke of a winter afternoon like turrets and pinnacles ... Twilight and night are the conditions under which to see an ironmaking town, the pillars of cloud by day, the pillars of fire by night.

The dynamism of the towns was, in the twenty years after the Great Exhibition, and partly inspired by the machinery exhibited at it, mirrored in the countryside. 'High farming'— capital spending on fertilizers, drainage, buildings, farm machinery such as reapers and threshers, roads linking with the new railways—apparently belied the argument that free trade spelt doom for the countryside, and led to considerable modernization, moral as well as physical, and even in the countryside there were fears for the continuance of traditional religion, as many turned to nonconformity and some to materialism.

An energetic and aggressive farming generation won the profits which maintained the sedate, leisured, county society depicted in Anthony Trollope's novels of Barsetshire. In 1868, 80 per cent of food consumed in the United Kingdom was still home-produced. But despite 'high farming', many areas, especially in Ireland and Scotland, remained woefully under-capitalized, the foot-plough and hand-winnowing still being common in the north and west Highlands in the early twentieth century.

URBAN POPULATION GROWTH 1841–1911

In the 1870s, a series of bad harvests, the opening of the North American prairies, faster and cheaper shipping thence and from the overseas wool-growing areas, led to 'the great depression'. Only milk, hay, and straw production were not open to harsh foreign competition. In particular, the price of grain, the characteristic product of the eastern side of the country, fell dramatically, but farmers, especially the smaller ones, were slow to accept the permanence of this fall, or to adapt to the new demand for dairy products. The pastoral west was less severely affected. The significance of agriculture in the economy declined as towns grew, a decline made swifter by the depression: in 1851 agriculture accounted for 20.3 per cent of the national income, in 1901 only 6.4 per cent, and the majority of British food and agricultural raw materials such as wool were imported—a fact which was to be of considerable strategic importance. Cries for the protection of agriculture received little response, even within the Tory Party—certainly not to the point of an alteration to the fiscal system of free trade. Some Liberal land reformers—for whom protection was axiomatically ruled out—advocated smallholdings (the 'three acres and a cow' campaign of 1885) as a solution; the establishment of the Crofting Commission (1886) for the Scottish Highlands, empowered to establish crofting communities free from landlord interference, was the only substantial achievement on the mainland, though a notable one in its long-term results.

The attraction of higher wages for fewer hours in the towns, mechanization in the 1850s and 1860s, depression in the last quarter of the century, all led to extensive rural depopulation—a great exodus mostly to the Scottish and English towns, some to the coalfields (especially in Wales), some to the colonies, some to the army. Between 1861 and 1901 the decrease in the total of rural male labourers in England and Wales was just over 40 per cent; the total of women, less easily employable in the towns, decreased less dramatically, leaving a marked imbalance of the sexes in the countryside, though many unmarried women found their way into domestic service in the towns aided by such agencies as the Girls' Friendly Society.

All this left rural society demoralized and neglected, with the passivity characteristic of communities in decay. Thomas Hardy's novels, whose span of publication (1872–96) covered almost exactly the years of the agricultural depression, captured majestically the uncontrollable and distant forces which seemed to determine the fate of the country communities and their inhabitants. Hardy wrote of country habits and traditions which had passed away but, though historical in form, the novels had a contemporary overtone. *The Mayor of Caster-bridge* described the fate of Michael Henchard, a corn merchant whose failure to adapt to new methods of trading brought him to ruin. Hardy observed of him at the moment of his financial crash: 'The movements of his mind seemed to tend to the thought that some power was working against him.' The 'general drama of pain' which the Wessex novels depict was the disintegration of a civilization. Surveying his novels as a whole in 1895 Hardy observed: 'The change at the root of this has been the recent supplanting of the class of stationary cottagers, who carried on the local traditions and humours, by a population of more or less migratory labourers, which has led to a break of continuity in local history, more fatal than any other thing to the preservation of legend, folk-lore, close intersocial relations, and eccentric individualities. For these the indispensable conditions of existence are attachment to the soil of one particular spot by generation after generation.' Fortunately, Cecil Sharp, Marjorie Kennedy-Fraser, and other folklore and folk-song and dance historians recorded something of the quality of British rural life before it was wholly lost.

The breaking up of country customs was encouraged by Whitehall and Westminster. Educational measures—for example the 1872 Scottish Education Act—worked to Anglicize the Gaelic-speakers of Scotland and Ireland and the Welsh-speakers of Wales, and to equip the peasantry for urban life. Between 1850 and 1900 rural change and education policy dealt those languages a powerful and in Scotland almost a fatal blow. In Wales, however, local initative secured the teaching of Welsh in schools from 1889.

In some areas, there was a good deal of movement between town and country, as migrant workers left the towns for the harvest, and poaching by the inhabitants of small towns in the surrounding countryside was common. Some industrial workers, especially coal-miners, lived in villages with moors and fields at their doors and their sports such as whippet and pigeon racing had rural associations. Middle-class people took advantage of low land values to buy up a country place. For the financially sharp members of the propertied classes, the countryside became an expensive playground, a place for 'week-ending'; but for many urban-dwellers in the great cities it became a remote, even dangerous, place populated by a curious people with antique accents, clothes, and manners. Oscar Wilde's comedy, *The Importance of Being Earnest* (1895), caught the metropolitan tone:

LADY BRACKNELL.... land has ceased to be either a profit or a pleasure. It gives one position, and prevents one from keeping it up. That's all that can be said about land.

JACK. I have a country house with some land, of course, attached to it, about fifteen hundred acres, I believe; but I don't depend on that for my real income. In fact, as far as I can make out, the poachers are the only people who make anything out of it.

LADY BRACKNELL. A country house! ... You have a town house, I hope? A girl with a simple, unspoilt nature, like Gwendolen, could hardly be expected to reside in the country.

None the less, the image of a happy rural past lingered in the town-dweller's mind: regardless of class, whenever he (or she) could, he lived in a house with a garden, and perhaps rented an allotment: he recreated the country in the town while ignoring the reality of its sufferings. Architecture and town-planning increasingly reflected nostalgia for the village, culminating in the Bournville experiment of Cadbury's, the Quaker employers, and in the 'Garden City' movement at the end of the century.

The Masses and the Classes: the Urban Worker

The urbanization of the mass of the population and the decline of rural areas not surprisingly had profound social consequences for all classes of the population. The greatest fear of the propertied classes in the first half of the century had been of a revolutionary working class or classes: that no such class emerged is perhaps the most striking feature of the second half of the century. Most industrial labourers left no memorial save the products of their labours: the details of their lives, their aspirations, hopes, beliefs, likes, dislikes, habits, and enthusiasms are largely lost. In the empire, detailed reports on all such things were drawn up with all the efficiency of the trained civil servant fascinated by an alien race, but at home it was only at the end of the century that systematic observation of the living customs of the British urban poor began. Henry Mayhew's impressionistic *London Labour and the London Poor: a Cyclopaedia of the Condition and Earnings of those that will work, those that cannot work, and those that will not work* (1861–2) made a start, but an unsystematic one, and one which was not followed up. What we do know suggests highly complex and varied patterns of life, with regionalism and religion often playing an important part.

The standard of living of some members of the labouring population began to increase quite fast. Between 1860 and 1914 real wages doubled. The years of particularly rapid growth were the boom years of 1868–74, and the period 1880–96; during the latter period real wages went up by almost 45 per cent. By the 1880s, for the first time in the century, a significant number began to enjoy leisure time. Some money (though not much) was coming to be available for more than the essentials of food, housing, and clothing. Strikingly, this surplus coincided not with a rise but with a fall in the birth-rate, which affected the propertied classes from the 1870s, the working classes, mirroring their social superiors, a little later. The extra cash was thus not absorbed by extra children. This was a startling and unprecedented development which falsified the predictions of the classical political economists from Malthus to Marx, that the labouring classes were condemned to subsistence levels of living through the 'iron law of wages' because any surplus wealth would be absorbed by extra children. Control of family size opened the way to the relative prosperity of the British working class since the 1880s. How and why this happened is hardly known. Men and women married later; they may have made some use of the rather unreliable birth-control devices popularized from the 1870s; women may have used abortion as a regular means of birth-prevention.

The term 'working classes' (the Victorians almost always used the plural) of course covered a wide spectrum. Charles Booth's survey of *Life and Labour of the People in London*, begun in the late 1880s, found six main categories: 'highpaid labour'; 'regular standard earnings'; 'small regular earnings'; 'intermittent earnings'; 'casual earnings'; and what Booth called the 'lowest class'. 'Regular standard earners' made up the largest group—as much as the total of the other five categories put together—and it was this group of men and women which particularly reduced the size of their families, saw their real incomes rise, and began to be aware of their potential power within the economy.

The growing prosperity of the 'regular standard earners' led them to join trade unions as a means of safeguarding their gains and of negotiating for better wages and conditions of work. The unions of the mid-century were for the most part rather narrowly-based 'craft unions', made up of men who jealously guarded the privileged and hard-won ascendancy among their fellow employees given them by their qualifications through apprenticeship or their responsibility for skilled machine-working. The steady demand for skilled labour reinforced the influence and status of the craft unions, and some technical developments, for example in the building of iron ships, expanded rather than diminished their importance. In the 1870s and especially in the 1880s these began to be supplemented to include many more of the workmen in regular employment. Rising living standards made this possible, for trade union membership was quite expensive. The unions existed not only, or even chiefly, for purposes of wage negotiation, but also for a wide variety of 'self-help' benefits and the trade unions were closely linked to, and sometimes synonymous with, the Friendly Societies. The first of these benefits for any self-respecting workman was the burial benefit—the avoidance of a funeral paid for by the workhouse—but many unions also had sickness and unemployment benefits, for the State as yet offered no help for victims of temporary calamity, still less did it assist those more permanently disadvantaged, save for the ultimate safety net of the workhouse.

Trade union activity grew in a context which seems most curious to the post-1945 observer. The twenty years after 1874 were characterized by a sharp and substantial deflation—that is, prices (and, to a lesser extent, wages) fell. On the other hand, *real* wages, for those in regular exployment, rose. But this was hard for trade unionists to come to terms with: a man will hardly believe that an employer who reduces his wages may still be leaving him better off. The new trade unionism was thus concerned to defend working-class wages: it was a reaction, as much as a positive force. It had little ideology except for the concept of solidarity. Some socialists played a part in the most publicized strikes of the period—the strike at Bryant and May's match factory in 1888, and the London Dock Strike for the 'dockers' tanner' in 1889, both of which attracted much middle-class interest, probably because they both occurred in London under the noses of the radicals. But these were not typical strikes (indeed the London Dock Strike was not conducted by a union: the union was formed *after* the strike finished); nor should the role of the 'socialists' who led them, such as John Burns, be over-stressed. Even most of the trade union leadership was staunchly Gladstonian: Karl Marx and his works were virtually unknown, outside a small circle, in the country where he had spent almost all his working life; the writings of the socialist groups which sprang up in the 1880s reached only a tiny audience. Indeed, the resistance of the working classes to socialist ideas made them the despair of middle-class intellectuals.

If the trade union was the institutional expression of a growing working-class self-awareness, shared leisure activities, especially for the male wage-earner, further encouraged this sense of solidarity. Watching Association Football—a game founded by public schools and university amateur clubs, but essentially professional by the mid-1880s—became the regular relaxation of males (and almost without exception only males) in industrial towns from Portsmouth to Aberdeen. In the last quarter of the nineteenth century a football club was established in every self-respecting industrial town. Some of these teams reflected the religious schisms of the cities (Catholic Celtic and Protestant Rangers in Glasgow, Catholic Everton and Protestant Liverpool on Merseyside). All of them encouraged a local patriotism, enthusiasm, and self-identification on the part of the followers, which was the envy of many a political organizer. Football was the product of a highly-organized urban society: the regularity and complexity of the Cup (from 1871) and League (from 1888) competitions, the need for sustained as well as immediate interest, the budgeting for the weekly entrance fee and, perhaps, train fare for the away match, the large, self-regulating crowds, all reflected a disciplined and ordered workforce, content to pay for its leisure watching *others* play for a club organized usually by local businessmen. Sustaining attention over the whole of the football 'season' gave the working man something of the wider perspective of time familiar to his agricultural counterpart from the climatic seasons.

The growing popularity of the much lengthier, more idiosyncratic and socially integrative game of cricket, organized through the County Championship from 1873, defies any such simple explanation; it was, perhaps, a testimony to the survival of individuality despite industrialization and the division of labour. W. G. Grace, the Gloucestershire physician whose autocratic command of the pitches and players of the day allowed him to set many batting, bowling, and fielding records still hardly surpassed, became almost as much of a national hero as Fred Archer, the champion jockey in 1874–86. Grace's great and much-caricatured beard caused him to be confused in the popular mind with Lord Salisbury—a confusion probably of some advantage to the latter.

Travel for the working class had hitherto taken place in the context of a desperate search for new employment or accommodation. By the 1880s it was starting to be recreational: the trip to the seaside organized individually or by the firm on one of the new Bank Holidays became for many an annual excursion. Resorts—Blackpool, Morecambe, Scarborough, Southend, Eastbourne, Portobello—rose to meet the demand and to stimulate it further. For the holidays of the working classes were almost always spent in towns: 'the beach' meant the pier, sideshows, and bathing cabins, backed by hotels, boarding houses, and shops. Radicals and socialists in the 1890s attempted to broaden this tradition through rambling and cycling clubs which made trips into the countryside, but the appeal of these was more to the lower middle class than to the working class.

The development of a popular press and the rapid nationwide communication made possible by the electric telegraph encouraged the other great working-class recreation: betting, especially on horses, and, through the nascent pools industry, on football. Betting offered the pot of gold at the end of the rainbow: leisure could be fun, but it might also be profitable—though, of course, it rarely was.

The more prosperous sections of the working classes thus began to share a little the prosperity and expectations which the industrial revolution had brought the propertied classes half a century earlier. Diets improved a little, with meat, milk, and vegetables in addition to bread, potatoes, and beer. The quality of housing was a little better; houses and people were cleaner as soap became cheaper and generally available. Books, photographs, the odd item of decorative furniture, began to adorn the regularly employed workman's home. Respectability, in the sense of having the use of money to demonstrate some degree of control of living style, some sense of settled existence, some raising of the horizon beyond the weekly wage packet, became a goal, encouraged by the spread of hire-purchase companies, which managed much of the spending of the working classes' surplus.

The rise in the standard of living of the wage-earning population was important, but it must be kept in perspective. The second half of the nineteenth century was punctuated by short-term dislocations of the economy in each decade. Many contemporaries believed that the years from the mid-1870s to the mid-1890s constituted a 'great depression', when profits fell. As we have seen, this phrase is certainly true with respect to agriculture. With respect to industry as a whole, it was a period of readjustment rather than depression, but for the working person 'readjustment' usually meant misery. It was during the 1880s that the word 'unemployment' was given its modern meaning.

Religion, in the sense of church-going, played little direct part in the life of most working people in the towns. 'It is not that the Church of God has lost the great towns; it has never had them,' wrote A. F. Winnington-Ingram (an Anglican clergyman) in 1896. Protestant churches both Anglican and nonconformist were unsuccessful in persuading rural labourers to continue as church-goers as they entered the towns, and they failed to reach the majority of those born in towns, despite the indirect allurements of charitable hand-outs and the provision of education in Sunday Schools, and the direct approach of missions, revival crusades, and the Salvation and Church Armies. In London in 1902–3 only about 19 per cent of the population regularly went to church, and those that did came largely from the socially superior areas. The figures would probably be a little better in provincial cities and considerably better in small towns. Only the Roman Catholics attracted significant working-class attendance: their organization was geared to this, and they skilfully appealed through church social organizations and clubs to the Irishness as much as to the Catholicism of their congregations.

This is not to say that the working classes were wholly ignorant of religion. 'Rites of passage' (especially weddings and funerals) remained popular even when secular alternatives became available. Nor do non-church-goers appear to have been actively hostile to religion except when it took on a Romish or ritualistic form and became linked with the abrasive relations between Irish immigrants and the host community. Rather, especially in the case of Anglicanism, they resented a religion so obviously linked to the status and power of the propertied classes. Not going to church, in a society whose articulate members so strongly advocated the practice, was a protest as well as a sign of indifference.

Clerks and Commerce: the Lower Middle Class

For the middle classes, the decades after 1850 offered a golden age of expansion. In 1851 the middle class was a fairly small and reasonably easily identified group: the professions, business men, bankers, large shopkeepers, and the like. The gulf between this group and the working classes was deep. By the end of the century, a far more complex pattern had emerged. A large, intermediate group, which may be called the lower middle class, was called into being by economic change. The service sector of the economy had become much greater and more complex. As the British economy became gradually as much commercial as industrial, it created a vast army of white-collar workers to manage and serve in the retailing, banking, accounting, advertising, and trading sectors. The management of factories passed from a paternal family tradition to a new class of professional managers, and the bureaucracies of manufacturing industry grew swiftly. The civil service, both local and central, began to expand rapidly as government spent more on new responsibilities, especially on the education system created by the Act of 1870. Shops, offices, and telephone exchanges offered new opportunities for the employment of women. London was particularly affected by the changes which created a vast army of City workers, trained at the new polytechnics, commuting by train or by the new underground railways from the suburbs being built on what was then the edge of the city, or from towns such as Croydon which developed rapidly from the 1870s as dormitories for City clerks. Suburbanization was the characteristic innovation of city life in the second half of the century: rows of neat houses, terraced or semi-detached, with small gardens, often both at front and rear of the house, testified to the successful propertied aspirations of this new society.

These were families which had done well out of the Liberal age: Liberalism called for individual achievement, and this class had responded. It valued merit, competition, respectability, efficiency, and a sense of purpose. It respected achievement, money, and success. Uncertain of its own position in the social order, it responded to those confident of their own right to command: it respected hierarchy. In this, it differed considerably from the sturdy individualism of Liberals in the 1850s, sustained by the pre-industrial ethos of 'the good old cause' and the rallying cries of the seventeenth century; its search for a secure place in the social order made it the vehicle by which the Conservatives became a party with a stake in the cities. In some places, particularly in small towns with a nonconformist tradition such as the market towns of Wales and Scotland, it ran the town, and the self-confidence this gave it, together with its nonconformity, helped to keep it Liberal. In large towns, it tended to act as a collaborating class, offering the aristocracy and the upper middle class the means of power in exchange for recognition and status.

The *Daily Mail*, founded by the Harmsworth brothers in 1896, with its highly efficient national distribution, soon had the provincial press on the run, and was the archetypal reading matter for the lower middle class; initially liberal–imperialist in tone, it crossed over to the Unionists during the Boer War. 'By office boys for office boys', Lord Salisbury contemptuously remarked of it and its clientele.

The Propertied Classes

The upper middle classes divided into two. Those working in the professions—doctors, lawyers, the clergy of the established church, civil servants of the administrative grade—shared a common background of education at university and, increasingly, at one of the public schools. In many towns, they lived more exclusively than in the first half of the century, moving out of the town centre to imposing villas in the suburbs. The habit of sending children away to boarding school increased the national outlook of this class and weakened the roots of its individual members in the localities. The spirit of Thomas Arnold of Rugby, as interpreted and modified by his successors, pervaded the outlook of the professions. Educated through a syllabus dominated by Greek, Latin, and ancient history, moralized at by Broad-Church Anglicanism, 'fitted for life' by incessant games (rugby football in the winter, cricket and athletics in the summer) designed to occupy every idle moment, the ethos of the professional classes was worthy but sterile. Increasingly designed to provide men to run an empire, it neglected the needs of an industrial state.

The manufacturing middle class was to some extent affected by this. Instead of sending their children early into the family firm, manufacturers increasingly sent them into the educational process designed for the professional classes. Sons of the owners of cotton mills and shipyards learnt Greek and rugby football, and not, as their German counterparts were doing, science and accounting. Sons educated in this way often showed little interest in returning to manufacturing life, and the preservation of the entrepreneurial and manufacturing ethos which had been one of the chief motors of industrial progress in the first half of the century became increasingly difficult. Such men found commerce more congenial than industry, and went into the expanding banking sector where the sweat and gore of the factory floor and labour relations were sterilized into columns of figures.

The British economy came to rely more and more on the competence of such men. A huge balance of payments deficit on imports and exports of commodities began to open (£27 million in 1851, £134 million by 1911). This was turned into an overall surplus by 'invisible earnings'—the profits of banking, insurance, shipping, and the income from British capital invested abroad. Income from services (£24 million in 1851, £152 million in 1911) and from overseas dividends (£12 million in 1851, £188 million in 1911) seemed to become the vital elements in British prosperity, and with them came a middle class whose chief expertise was in handling money, not men or products.

This important development in British social and economic life was as unplanned as the earlier phase of manufacturing industrialization. It was the product of that industrialization in two ways. As the 'workshop of the world' sold its products abroad, it stimulated other economies which cried out for capital they could not themselves supply. Competition with such economies, and depression in some sectors of manufacturing in the 1880s, lowered the rate of profit on British manufacturing, and the 'invisible hand' thus pointed the way to the expansion of the service industries.

Again, this tendency must not be exaggerated, nor its novelty over-stressed. The easy fusion of land, industry, and commerce was a well-established English tradition. It had prevented the aristocracy becoming a caste in the Continental style, and it had offered the reward of status to the manufacturer. Some took this reward, others, especially nonconformists, did not seek it. Manufacturing and manufacturers remained a powerful force in England. But the primacy of manufacturers, 'the monarchy of the middle classes', so much expected and feared in the first half of the century, did not occur. In part this must be explained by the extent to which the aristocracy neutralized the political and social effects of 'trade' by absorbing it.

The middle classes were Protestant, and actively so. They were increasingly important within the hierarchy of the Anglican Church and the universities: the latter now catered largely for them as the passing of professional and civil-service examinations became required through the series of reforms consequent upon the Northcote–Trevelyan Report of 1854. Respectability, the need to maintain the house, and to pay the servants and school and university fees, encouraged restriction in the size of middle-class families from the 1870s, that is, rather earlier than the same phenomenon among the working classes.

Smaller families were also sought by middle-class women who were beginning to expect more from life than the privilege of breeding children and running the household. Women, thus partially liberated, played an important role in charities, churches, local politics, and the arts, especially music. With great difficulty, some forced themselves upon the universities (they were allowed to attend lectures and take examinations, but not degrees), and from the late 1870s women's colleges were founded at Oxford, Cambridge, and London. The professions remained barred to women, but a few succeeded in practising as doctors. The upper levels of nursing were, however, the nearest most women could get to a professional career.

Pomp and Circumstance

The aristocracy (and gentry) was only partly affected by these changes. Of the three great classes in British social life, it probably changed the least in Victoria's reign. The aristocracy was, as the socialist writer Beatrice Webb observed, 'a curiously tough substance'. It continued to wield considerable political power, supplying much of the membership of both political parties at Westminster, occupying almost all the upper posts in the empire, running local government in the counties, and officering the army—the navy was less socially exclusive. The aristocracy and gentry gained from prosperous farming in the 1850s–1870s, and lost by the agricultural depression; but it recovered some of its losses by skilful investment in urban land, and by the windfall of urban expansion, as what had been agricultural lands of declining value made their owners wealthy as suburbs were built upon them. The British aristocracy had always been involved in industrialization, especially in the development of mining, canals, and railways. It now shrewdly associated itself with the new wave of commercial expansion: most banks and insurance companies had a Lord to add tone to the managerial board. It also shored up its fortunes by astute marriages, notably with the new aristocracy of wealth in the United States: the best-known example was the marriage of the ninth duke of Marlborough to Consuelo Vanderbilt. By these means, many of the great aristocratic estates were preserved despite agricultural decline. But they were playthings as much as engines of wealth, and came to be treated as such. The aristocracy came to be known to the urban population chiefly through their representation in the popular press and magazines as men and women of leisure: racing, hunting, shooting and fishing in the country, gambling and attending the season in London. In a population for which leisure was becoming increasingly important, this did not make the aristocracy unpopular. The court led the way. The gravity which Albert applied to court life in the south was applied with equal pertinacity to the serious business of recreation in the north. Victoria and Albert's development of Balmoral on Deeside in the 1850s, their obvious and highly publicized enjoyment of peasant life and lore, their patronage of Sir Edwin Landseer, the hugely popular artist of rural slaughter, made Scotland respectable, and likewise similar moors and mountains in the north and west of England and in Wales. The court linked itself to the Romantic movement, now in its declining and consequently most popular phase, and by doing so re-established its popularity and represented the control of nature by an urban civilization. *The Monarch of the Glen*, Landseer's portrait of a stag, one of the most reproduced of all Victorian paintings, is not monarch of all he surveys, but a stag at bay, within the gun sights of the stalker: no glen was safe, nature was tamed.

Victoria and Albert's life at Balmoral was enjoyable but high-minded: duty to the peasantry was consistently emphasized. The Prince of Wales, Victoria's son Edward who succeeded her in 1901, was merely hedonistic. A series of scandals alarmed his mother but gratified the press by the copy they yielded. The Prince with his coterie of rich friends such as Sir Thomas Lipton, who made a fortune from the new retail trade in groceries, epitomized the 'plutocracy'. The evangelicalism and tractarianism which made such a mark on the aristocracy in post-Regency days and which made Palmerston's dandyism in the 1850s and 1860s seem conspicuously out of place, appeared to give way to ostentatious consumption and a general moral laxity. Some aristocrats, such as Lord Salisbury, the Tory Prime Minister, continued the old fashion of simple living despite magnificent surroundings, with a household noted for its religious tone. But Salisbury, the last Prime Minister to wear a beard, was becoming an anachronism by his last decade, the 1890s. Arthur Balfour, his nephew and successor as Prime Minister, was seen as a free-thinker. Balfour and Edward VII characterized the new fashion—the one apparently sceptical, the other openly sybaritic.

Despite the marked difference in style between Victoria and her son, the monarchy—the apex of the court and of polite society generally—flourished under both. Victoria in her long reign (1837–1901) jealously guarded its prerogatives which increasingly she saw as best safeguarded by a Conservative government. Her long disappearances from public life after Albert's death in 1861 were unpopular, and made possible quite a serious republican movement stimulated by the Paris Commune, which was headed off with some skill by the Liberal Party leadership in the early 1870s. It was the absence and idleness of the monarch that caused widespread adverse comment, not her presence. In a rapidly-changing society with important elements strongly receptive to the appeal of hierarchy, the monarchy, carefully presented by the growing mass-communications industry, seemed something of a fixed point, with its emphasis on family, continuity, and religion. Walter Bagehot in his classic study, *The English Constitution* (1867), pointed out that the English 'defer to what we may call the *theatrical show* of society . . . the climax of the play is the Queen'. The monarchy helped to legitimize power: it is 'commonly hidden like a mystery, and sometimes paraded like a pageant', as it was with great success at the Jubilees in 1887 and 1897. The obvious ordinariness of Victoria herself, her well-publicized sufferings ('the widow of Windsor', bravely performing her duties), and the fact that she was a woman, old and often ill, pointed up the contrast between human frailty and the majesty of institutions, much increasing respect for the latter.

The monarchy represented the timeless quality of what was taken to be a pre-industrial order. In an increasingly urbanized society, it balanced the Industrial Revolution: the more urban Britain became, the more stylized, ritualized, and popular became its monarchy, for the values which it claimed to personify stood outside the competitive egalitarianism of capitalist society.

'A Great Change in Manners'

Britain (with the exception of Ireland) between the 1850s and the 1890s was a society of remarkable order and balance, given its extraordinary underlying tensions of industrial and social change. Though political rioting did not altogether disappear, it became infrequent enough to encourage widespread comment. Crime on the mainland, both in the form of theft and of acts of violence, declined absolutely as well as relatively—an extraordinary development in a rapidly-expanding population, firmly contradicting the adage that industrialization and urbanization necessarily lead to higher rates of criminality. The Criminal Registrar noted in 1901 that, since the 1840s, 'we have witnessed a great change in manners: the substitution of words without blows for blows with or without words; an approximation in the manners of different classes; a decline in the spirit of lawlessness.' This largely self-regulating society relied on voluntary organizations—the Churches, the Friendly Societies, a vast network of charitable organizations—to cater for spiritual and physical deprivation. In one important area—education—it was already admitted by the 1860s that voluntary effort by the Churches could not supply an elementary education system adequate to the needs of an industrial state, and in 1870 the Liberal government passed an Act to set up Education Boards with a duty to build board schools where there were no church schools (though children were not *required* to attend them until 1880, and had to pay to do so until 1891). Local initiative, especially in London and some of the northern manufacturing towns, grafted on to the elementary schools a quite effective and wide-ranging system of technical education for teenagers and even adults—but because it depended on the imagination of each school board, this system was patchy and in no way matched its German equivalent. Manufacturing towns, notably Manchester and Birmingham, set up civic universities much less orientated towards a classical education for those entering the traditional professions than Oxford and Cambridge. Government responsibility for education was seen by contemporaries as one of Mill's exceptions to the rule, not as the start of a wider acceptance of responsibility for social organization.

'Villa Tories': the Conservative Resurgence

By increasing the electorate from 20 per cent to 60 per cent of adult men in the towns, and to 70 per cent in the counties, the Reform Acts of 1867 and 1884 posed problems for politicians.

Household suffrage presented them with a much larger, though by no means universal, body of voters (far short of a universal suffrage, even for men) and elections were by secret ballot, whereas previously each individual's vote had been published.

For the Liberal coalition, accustomed never to losing general elections, the question was, could their amorphous system of informal alliances continue to be successful? It was a question posed the more starkly when Gladstone's first government disintegrated in the traditional Liberal style in 1873–4, and then, untraditionally, lost the election, thus yielding power to the Tories for the first time since 1846. The Liberals' response was twofold. In certain urban areas, and especially in Birmingham, where Joseph Chamberlain was the dominant political figure, a tight 'caucus' system of party organization was introduced. The 'caucus' was a group of self-appointed local notables, often nonconformist business men, and usually strongly critical of the Liberal Party leadership as being too cautious and too aristocratic. The National Liberal Federation, formed in 1877, attempted to give a degree of bureaucratic unity to the sundry local caucuses. On the other hand, the Liberal leadership, still predominantly aristocratic, reacted with alarm. Spanning the two groups was the commanding figure of W. E. Gladstone, son of a Liverpool (originally Scottish) corn merchant, but educated at Eton and Christ Church, Oxford; himself strongly Anglican but in the later phases of his career sympathetic to nonconformist aspirations, he was thus able to appeal to a wide spectrum of Victorian society. Gladstone had no 'caucus' to back him up: he aspired to a national rather than a local basis of power. He appealed over the heads of the local organizations to the body of Liberal opinion at large, and his means was the political speech and pamphlet. The new and vast network of national and provincial newspapers, linked by the telegraph, allowed for the first time an instant national debate: a politician's speech could be on the breakfast table of every middle-class household in the land the morning after it was given. Thus in the general election campaign of 1868, in his campaign against the Disraeli government's supine reaction to massacres of Christians by Turks in Bulgaria in 1876, and in his campaign against the moral and financial delinquency of the imperialistic exploits of the Conservatives in 1879–80 (the 'Midlothian Campaign'), Gladstone blazed a new trail in an attempt to create a great popular front of moral outrage. 'The Platform' became the characteristic form of late Victorian politics: Gladstone invented a new forum of political debate, and his contemporaries, both Liberal and Tory, were obliged to join in.

The 1867 Reform Act brought the Tories new opportunities. Accustomed, almost habituated to losing, they began to win. In 1867 the National Union of Conservative and Constitutional Associations was founded, and in 1870 a Central Office began to improve the co-ordination of electoral strategy. The target for the Tories was the boroughs: to obtain political power they had to enlarge their base from the counties to the expanding towns and suburbs. This they did with very considerable success in the 1870s and 1880s. Under the leadership of Disraeli they won the general election of 1874 convincingly; under the leadership of Salisbury after Disraeli's death in 1881 they became the predominant party. They achieved this by linking an essentially hierarchic, aristocratic, and Anglican party with the aspirations of the expanding middle and lower middle classes in the great cities: the Tories became the party of property and patriotism. Disraeli saw that political success was becoming as much a question of presentation as of policy. In famous speeches in Lancashire and at the Crystal Palace in 1872, he portrayed the Liberals as unpatriotic, a danger to property, a threat to the institutions of the nation, betrayers of Britain's world and imperial interests. In a more positive vein, he advocated a policy of social reform, supposedly of particular appeal to such members of the working classes as had recently become voters. The themes of these speeches—especially the patriotic ones—were quickly taken up by other Conservatives. They were the prototype for most Tory election addresses for the next century.

The early years of the Conservative government of 1874–80 were marked by a burst of social reforms mostly promoted by R. A. Cross, the Home Secretary: artisans' dwellings, public health, Friendly Societies, river pollution, the sale of food and drugs, merchant shipping, trade unions, factories, drink licensing, and education were all the subject of legislation. Many of these reforms were 'in the pipeline' and owed a strong debt to the Peelite–Liberal traditions which had also motivated the previous Gladstone government. They affected middle-class perhaps more than working-class interests and because the social measures were permissive rather than compulsory their effect was more limited than might have been expected (for example, by 1880, only ten of eighty-seven Welsh and English towns had decided to implement the Artisans' Dwellings Act). None the less, these reforms were important in Conservative mythology. They showed that the Tories could be a party which dealt effectively with urban questions, and they offered the basis for the claim that 'Tory democracy' was a reality. Contrasted with German conservative answers to the problems of urban life, they appeared integrative, conciliatory, and constructive.

But the real interest of Conservatism was the consolidation of an urban middle-class base: working-class support was a bonus. The bogy of Liberal lack of patriotism was only partially successful, for the Tories' claim to be the party of competent imperialism was severely dented by their mishandling of events in South Africa and Afghanistan in the late 1870s, and by the high costs of their military exploits. It was hard simultaneously to be imperialists and to appeal to the middle-class virtue of financial retrenchment: a self-contradiction which Gladstone's Midlothian speeches skilfully exposed.

The Tories lost the 1880 general election, borne down partly by Gladstone's oratory, partly by the trade recession of that year. The succeeding Gladstone government of 1880–5 was the nadir of Liberalism, the party restless, the Cabinet divided. In imperial affairs, Tory claims seemed borne out: hesitation and confusion led to a series of disasters, culminating in the death of Charles Gordon at Khartoum in 1885. Too habituated to the way the 'official mind' of the colonial office thought to decline to extend imperial responsibilities, the Liberals occupied territory while declaring their regrets: electorally, they lost both ways, alienating anti-imperialists by doing too much, and imperialists by seeming reluctant. In domestic affairs, Gladstone's determination to control and reduce expenditure made positive reform difficult. In marked contrast to 1868–74, the government was noted for only one great reform, the county franchise reform of 1884. The enfranchisement of agricultural labourers was expected to deliver the county seats into the Liberals' hands and Salisbury used the blocking power of the House of Lords to extract a great prize as a 'tit-for-tat': a redistribution bill allowed the boundaries of borough seats to be drawn much more favourably to the Tories. Thus the Tories were able to use a Liberal reform to create a political structure of single-member, middle-class urban and suburban constituencies on which the basis of their subsequent political success has since consistently rested.

The effect of this was to make the Liberals increasingly dependent on the 'Celtic fringe', the Irish, Scottish, and Welsh MPs. The concerns and priorities of these three countries thus moved on to the centre of the British imperial stage.

Ireland, Scotland, Wales: Home Rule Frustrated

That there was an 'Irish problem', nobody could deny: what it was, hardly anybody could agree. Disraeli caught the tone of metropolitan bewilderment:

I want to see a public man come forward and say what the Irish question is. One says it is a physical question; another, a spiritual. Now it is the absence of the aristocracy, then the absence of railroads. It is the Pope one day, potatoes the next.

Irish agriculture was overwhelmingly the country's largest industry and was overwhelmingly owned by Protestants, who mostly, contrary to popular myth, lived on or near their estates. It flourished in the boom of the 1850s and 1860s and achieved a modest degree of technical improvement, but it remained, compared with England, grossly under-capitalized. Ireland could not produce her own capital, and could not attract much from England. Her economy could not sustain her population: unknown numbers moved to the mainland, where no town of any size was without its Irish community; between 1841 and 1925 gross 'overseas' emigration included four and three-quarter million to the USA, 70,000 to Canada, and more than 370,000 to Australia.

The legacy of the 1798 rebellion, the failure of Daniel O'Connell's attempt in the 1830s and 1840s to repeal the 1800 Act of Union, and the catastrophe of the famine of 1845–6, produced the Fenian Irish independence movement of the 1860s which attempted risings in the USA and in Canada and in Ireland. In 1867 it astonished England by a series of bomb explosions, notably one at Clerkenwell Prison in London, in which over one hundred innocent persons were killed. The Fenian movement in no sense represented Irish opinion generally, but the danger that it might come to do so encouraged Liberal politicians, especially Gladstone, to concessionary action. Disestablishment of the Anglican Church in Ireland in 1869, the Land Act of 1870, and an abortive educational reform in 1873 (rejected by the Irish members themselves) were intended to show that Westminster could give the mass of the Irish what they wanted. But these reforms were not enough. Isaac Butt's Home Government Association flourished, and the Liberal Party, hitherto the dominant party in Irish politics, was on the run. The agricultural depression from the early 1870s to the mid 1890s greatly worsened the situation. Charles Stewart Parnell (like Butt, a Protestant) became leader of the Home Rule Party in 1877, a position he held until his ruin in a divorce scandal in 1890. Parnell was prepared to exploit every political situation without reluctance or embarrassment—but even this tougher line was to some extent outflanked by the Land League which sought personal ownership of the land for the peasantry. Parnell, somewhat ambivalently, became its president in 1879. The Land League—a potent blend of 'physical force' Fenians and 'moral force' Parnellites fused into a popular front of nationalistic Catholicism—fought a sustained campaign against evictions in the 'Land War' of 1879–82 at the height of the depression, meeting them with violence and their perpetrators with 'boycotting' (named after Captain Charles Boycott, whose nerve cracked when faced with social and economic ostracism). Violence in the Irish countryside, and the murder in 1882 of the Irish secretary, Lord Frederick Cavendish, Gladstone's nephew by marriage, astonished and appalled the propertied classes in England which, as we have seen, had become accustomed to a very low level of violent crime.

The Gladstone Government of 1880 met this crisis on the one hand with coercion and on the other with concession, in the form of the 1881 Land Act, which gave much to the peasants, but did not give them ownership. The Home Rule Party increased its hold on Ireland (helped by the county franchise reform of 1884) and at the election of December 1885 won 86 seats, thus holding the balance of power between the Liberals and Tories at Westminster.

Gladstone cut the Gordian knot by coming out for Home Rule; a private appeal to Salisbury to treat the question on a bipartisan basis was rejected. Gladstone's decision was quite consistent with the main thrust of Liberal thinking, but its timing recognized political necessity: only once subsequently, in 1906, were the Liberals to gain power without the need for the support of Home Rule MPs in the lobbies. Most Liberals championed devolution and the rights of nations 'struggling rightly to be free', as Gladstone put it; it was hard to deny in 1886 that Ireland had proved itself to be such a nation. The question was, was its nationality to be recognized or crushed? Moreover, the moderate Home Rule Bill produced by Gladstone in 1886 did not grant independence, though it was the argument of its opponents first, that despite Parnell's assurances it would in the long run lead to Irish independence, and, second, that it gave no safeguard against 'Rome Rule' to the Protestant population, mostly concentrated in Belfast, the industrial capital of the province of Ulster.

This complex series of events led to a major crisis in British politics. The Liberal Party, faced with Gladstone's Home Rule Bill in the summer of 1886, split: 93 MPs, most of them Whigs under Lord Hartington but with some radicals under Joseph Chamberlain, voted with the Tories against the bill, thus bringing down the Liberal government and introducing twenty years of Conservative (or Unionist, as the anti-Home Rule Coalition was called) hegemony. With the Liberal-Unionists (the defectors from Liberalism) went a significant proportion of the Liberal press and almost all those landed aristocrats who traditionally paid most of the party's electoral expenses. This loss of influence and money was probably of more importance to the Liberals than the actual numbers of defecting MPs, though in the Lords the Liberals were now a tiny minority.

The split of 1886 weakened the party, but left Gladstone in control of it and of the National Liberation Federation, a hold he consolidated at its Newcastle meeting in 1891 when he accepted its radical programme. Home Rule thus shackled Liberalism to Gladstone. Before 1886, Ireland blocked the way to the passage of second-rank measures, so Home Rule was necessary as well as right. But after 1886, Home Rule was impossible, given the existence of the House of Lords. Home Rule thus both stimulated Liberals to battle for the right, and condemned them to a generation of frustration.

Naturally enough, events in Ireland affected Scotland and Wales. In both, disestablishment of the Church also became a political issue, and both experienced land campaigns. These had little of the violence characteristic of parts of Ireland, though in the Isle of Skye troops were used in 1882 to suppress crofter demonstrations. Certain Liberals in both countries demanded 'Home Rule All Round' and this movement, buoyed up by the cultural renaissance that Wales and Scotland shared with Ireland in the late nineteenth century, achieved considerable influence in the Liberal Party in the late 1880s and 1890s. Unlike Ireland, however, the Liberal Party was able to contain within itself the quasi-nationalistic movements in Scotland and Wales, partly because the dominant industrial sector in Scotland and the growing predominance in Wales of the South Wales coalfield bound those countries far more intimately than Ireland to the imperial economy; in southern Scotland and South Wales Liberal imperialism trumped nationalism.

With the Liberal Party split, and unable to reunite despite various attempts in the late 1880s, the Tories consolidated their hold. They were not active reactionaries. Salisbury made no attempt to reverse the Liberal achievements of the 1850s–1870s which at the time he had so bitterly opposed. Their position and their alliance with the Liberal-Unionists depended on preventing things being done, not on doing them. Thus though some legislation was passed, particularly the establishment of elected County Councils in 1888, a measure to improve working-class housing in 1890, and, later, the Education Act of 1902, which went some way to establishing a system of secondary education, the Unionist hegemony of 1886–1905 was not a period of legislative significance, nor was it intended to be. The urban electorate which the Tories essentially relied upon wanted the continuation of the Liberal state of the 1850s and 1860s, without the new accretions to Liberalism such as Home Rule. It rejected Gladstonian Liberalism, not because it had turned its back on the gains of the free-trade years in the mid-century, but because the Gladstonian Liberals seemed to have progressed too far beyond the objectives of that period. The anti-Gladstonian coalition thus relied heavily on Home Rule to keep the coalition together and to keep the Liberals out. It ventured beyond its anti-Home Rule stance at its electoral peril, as it was to find out in the early years of the twentieth century. The continuing Liberal commitment to Home Rule helped in this. The short Liberal minority government of 1892–5 (Gladstone's last administration, with

Rosebery as its Prime Minister after his retirement in 1894) spent much effort upon the second Home Rule Bill, which it succeeded in passing through the Commons only to see it thrown out by the Lords. The Liberals could mount a disparate majority made up of the English counties, Scotland, Wales, and Ireland, but they could not sustain it or repeat it. The Unionists won convincingly in 1895 and confirmed their majority in 1900, taking advantage of temporary successes in the South African war to hold the 'Khaki election'.

Reluctant Imperialists?

The Unionist case against Home Rule had always had an imperial dimension: imperial power must not be devolved, the very circumstances of the passing of the Act of Union in 1800 showing the strategic importance of Ireland, which Home Rule would again put at risk. In the last third of the century, imperial issues became much more of a public preoccupation; we must now look at their effect on Britain's position in the world.

The British did not as a whole look for increased direct imperial authority, and pressure groups for its extension were of little popular or political significance. Indeed, in the old areas of white settlement, they successfully sought to devolve authority, passing the Dominion of Canada Act in 1867 and the Commonwealth of Australia Act in 1900. Yet the last forty years of the century saw the annexation of vast areas of land in Africa, the Far East, and the Pacific. In 1851 Britain was the world's trader, with an overwhelming dominance of world shipping, which continued even when Britain's dominance in manufactured goods was declining after 1870. British interests were thus to be found wherever there was trade, even though British imperial authority might not be *formally* present. *Informal* imperialism thus preceded formal annexation: nothing could be less true than the adage, 'trade follows the flag'. In almost every case, it was the opposite. As Joseph Conrad's novels illustrate, there was no creek, however distant, without its British representative, organizing the shipping of paraffin oil and local goods.

In East and Central Africa, the first European presence was often religious, as evangelical medical missionaries such as David Livingstone preached the gospel, healed the sick, and exposed the inhumanity of the inland slave trade. H. M. Stanley's 'rescue' of Livingstone in 1871, skilfully self-publicized, became one of the great adventure stories of Victorian times, and greatly increased interest in 'the dark continent.'

In some areas, British attempts to trade were supported by arms—a notable example being the opium monopoly of the Indian government and the general free-trading access which was forced upon the Chinese government by the British in a series of 'opium wars' culminating in the treaty of Tien-tsin (1858), the most disreputable of all Britain's imperialistic exploits, because it was a considered and consistent policy, not the accidental result of a local crisis. Governmental involvement of an oblique sort was sometimes used to develop small beginnings through the device of the Chartered Company—a trading company with governmentally guaranteed rights to trade and administer an area; Nigeria, East Africa, and Rhodesia all came under eventual British rule in this way, for when a Company went bankrupt (or effectively so—Cecil Rhodes's British South Africa Company never paid a dividend before 1920 and was taken over in 1923) the British government had little option but to assume its administrative responsibilities.

In addition to this huge and largely informal network of trade was the centre-piece of India, 'the chief jewel in the imperial crown', now no longer so profitable, but the assumed focal point of British thinking about security outside the European context. Following the Indian mutiny of 1857–8, the old East India Company was wound up, and its territories came under direct British administration. In 1876, at the express wish of the queen, an Act was passed at Westminster which declared her 'Empress of India'.

To safeguard India, and the route to that subcontinent,

THE EXPANSION
OF THE
BRITISH EMPIRE
1815–1914

CANADA

NEWFOUNDLAND

· Bermuda·

Bahamas·

·BR. HONDURAS·

Jamaica·

St Lucia·
Barbados·
Tobago·
Trinidad·

·Mosquito Coast
(British until 1850)

BRITISH
GUIANA

Falkland Is

Bermuda· Extent by 1815
Gilbert Is Additions to 1914

various annexations were made. In the vicinity, Burma and
Malaysia were annexed, largely at the urging of the government
of India in Calcutta, which conducted its own programme
of imperialism with the systematic approach characteristic of
everything it did, and quite dissimilar to the haphazard
methods of London. On the route, Egypt and the Sudan came
under British control, and imperial expansion in East and South
Africa was at least partly affected by Indian considerations.
This simple statement of course disguises an extremely complex
narrative with respect to each of these annexations. The most
controversial annexations were in Egypt and South Africa, and
some attention should be given to these.

The route to India had made security in the eastern
Mediterranean, especially against Russia, a long-standing Brit-
ish preoccupation. Between 1854 and 1856 the British and
French, with some assistance from Piedmont-Sardinia, had sent

substantial fleets and armies to prop up Turkey. The Crimean
War had a complex series of causes, but the root one was
Russian aggrandizement against the sprawling and feeble Ottoman Empire. The performance of Britain and France, the two
most 'advanced' European nations, against 'backward' Russia
was disappointing and in certain respects inept, although the
supply by sea of large armies at a considerable distance created
new problems. The newspaper-reporting by telegraph of the
hardships of the troops starkly illustrated the problems and the
paradox of war-making by a liberal state, and Florence Night-
ingale made a name for herself as the 'lady with the lamp'. The
immobility of the campaign, which consisted largely of a series
of sieges, bloodily resolved in the Crimea and in the area of
Kars in Asiatic Turkey, looked forward to the 1914–18 war.
Turkey was successfully defended, and the British thus shored
up the Ottoman Empire of which Egypt was a part.

The hope was that Turkey would reform and behave like a modern, liberal state. This hope was not fulfilled. By the 1870s, Turkey was again disintegrating, and under attack from Russia. The Disraeli government of 1874–80 continued the Crimean policy of defending Turkish integrity: the Liberal opposition under Gladstone argued that this was no longer feasible and supported the division of much of 'Turkey in Europe' into separate, Christian states. The 'Concert of Europe' present at the Congress of Berlin in 1878 reached agreement on this and Disraeli returned to London bringing 'peace with honour' and the imperial gain of the island of Cyprus, thought to be of strategic importance for the Eastern Mediterranean, but in fact useless as a naval base.

As Turkey disintegrated, so Egypt became increasingly self-reliant, organizing the building of the Suez Canal, opened in 1870, and of great importance to Britain's links with India. The inflow of capital to build the canal destabilized Egypt, which began to disintegrate socially and politically. In 1875 Disraeli bought the Khedive's large holding in the shares of the company which ran the canal. Thus when Egypt reached the point of bankruptcy, and a military coup was attempted, Britain had not only a general strategic interest in the situation but also a direct financial one. After attempts to find alternatives, Gladstone reluctantly invaded and occupied Egypt on behalf of the canal's creditors in 1882, and the British remained until 1954, though the country was never formally annexed and was thus similar in status to the theoretically independent princely states in India. Formal annexation of the rebellious Sudan naturally followed in a series of campaigns in the 1880s and 1890s, the Mahdi, the slayer of the maverick Gordon in 1885, being finally and ruthlessly crushed by Kitchener at the battle of Omdurman in 1898. Turkish decay thus drew Britain into becoming the major power in the Eastern Mediterranean and in North-eastern Africa.

Events in South Africa were not dissimilar, but were complicated by the presence of the Boers. The Cape was occupied in 1795 to safeguard the route to India. The security of the hinterland, whither the Boers had trekked in the 1830s, affected the Cape. Various plans for incorporating the Boers in a federation were suggested, and confederation was imposed upon the Boers by the Disraeli government in 1877 at a moment when the Boers were weakened by the Zulus. Incompetent generalship (a feature of British military operations in South Africa) led to the death of 800 British troops at Isandhlwana, one of the very few occasions in colonial wars in which spears triumphed over guns. This was, of course, only a temporary set-back, and the Zulus were liquidated at Ulundi (1879). The Boers then wished to regain their independence. After a short war when the defeat of a small group of British soldiers at Majuba Hill in 1881 gave a propaganda value to the Boers out of all proportion to its military significance, an ill-defined agreement was reached: the Transvaal and Orange Free State to have independence, but under British suzerainty. Increasing exploitation of diamonds and the discovery of gold in the Transvaal in 1886 transformed the situation. In financial terms, Southern Africa became literally Britain's chief imperial jewel. The influx of capital directed by men such as Cecil Rhodes destabilized the rural economy of the Boers, as it had that of Egypt. The Transvaal, like Egypt, went bankrupt, but the Boers, under Paul Kruger, retained strict political control. An attempt by Dr Jameson, a crony of Rhodes, to encourage a rising by the Uitlanders (the British in the Transvaal without political rights) failed in 1896. Alfred Milner, the new High Commissioner, asserted British rights over the Boer republics and determined to break Kruger by war. Milner goaded Kruger into attacking Cape Colony in 1899, and what was expected to be a short, limited war began. The Boers, however, were well stocked with German arms; the British, used to fighting colonial wars against undisciplined natives without guns, proceeded ineptly, and a series of disasters followed before weight of armaments captured the main Boer cities in 1900. The war seemed over, and Chamberlain, the Colonial Secretary, persuaded Salisbury to hold the 'Khaki election', easily won by the

Unionists. But the Boers refused to accept defeat, and harassed the British with guerrilla tactics. The British replied by burning Boer farms, clearing the veldt, and systematically herding Boer families into 'concentration camps'. High death-rates in the camps led to radical protests in Britain. 'When is a war not a war?' asked Sir Henry Campbell-Bannerman, Rosebery's successor as Liberal leader, answering himself: 'When it is carried on by methods of barbarism in South Africa'. In 1902, peace was negotiated: Milner had failed in his aim of smashing the social and political structure of Afrikanerdom.

The fin-de-siècle *Reaction: New Views of the State*

The Boer War was immensely expensive, costing far more than all Britain's other imperial exploits in the nineteenth century put together. It failed to smash the Boers, but it did smash the Gladstonian system of finance, raising government expenditure to a new plateau from which it never descended. The war also put into stark and dramatic popular form a number of concerns which were already preoccupying the intelligentsia. The war showed the strength and loyalty of the empire, for the white colonies sent troops to help, but it also showed its weaknesses. The empire seemed over-extended and under-coordinated. The British navy was no longer pre-eminent. The French navy was being joined as a threat by the Germans, the Italians, the Americans, and the Japanese. The policy of 'splendid isolation' began to look dangerous. Imperial rivalry had meant that in the 1870s–1890s France had usually seemed Britain's most likely enemy and Germany her most likely friend. Germany's navy plan of 1898, and her bid for 'a place in the sun' which coincided with her encouragement to Kruger during the Boer War, now made Germany seem a potent threat, the contemporary feeling about which is well captured in Erskine Childers's classic spy story *The Riddle of the Sands* (1903). Naval security in the Indian Ocean and the Pacific was gained by the Anglo-Japanese alliance of 1902. This attempt to limit imperial responsibility was followed up by agreements (*Ententes*) resolving imperial differences with France in 1904 over North Africa and with Russia in 1907 over Persia. The Boer War thus led to a 'new course' in British foreign policy. For while these *Ententes* were formally about extra-European areas, their real importance came to lie within Europe; although they were not alliances, they committed Britain, to some extent, to the side of the Franco-Russian alliance against Germany and Austria in the rising tension in Europe. What that extent was, was not yet clear.

Anxieties about world security raised by the Boer War also popularized discussion about Britain's relative economic position, for it was upon that that national strength ultimately rested. The overwhelming superiority of the British economy of the 1850s was much diminished. The USA, Germany, France, and Russia were now all substantial industrial powers, with the first two superior to the British in certain sectors of their economies. Britain was now one among several, no longer the unaccompanied trail-blazer. Yet for the most part British society and government behaved as if nothing had changed. The liberal state of the 1850s and 1860s, with its precepts of free trade, minimal government spending, an economy autonomous and self-regulating, lingered on, almost as carefully guarded under Conservative as under Liberal management. The *per capita* expenditure of central government in 1851 was £2.00; by 1891 it had only increased to £2.50 (by 1913 it was to be £4.00). In the 1880s and 1890s this situation came under increasing criticism, much of which the Boer War seemed to confirm and popularize.

Slow military progress in the Crimean War of the 1850s led to criticism of the competence of the ruling élite; military ineffectiveness and the poor quality of recruits in the South African war led to a public cry among the propertied classes for a reappraisal of the economic, social, and even political arrangements of the nation as a whole.

Before considering the various schools of criticism of traditional Liberalism, a general influence should be noted, that of 'social Darwinism'. We saw earlier that positivists were strong supporters of *laissez-faire*. In the 1880s and 1890s the influence of social Darwinism began to take a different form. The struggle for 'the survival of the fittest' began to be seen less in terms of individuals in the market-place and more in terms of competition between nations. This dramatically reduced the number of units under discussion, and raised the question, prompted also by the imperialism which was related to this national competition, of whether individual 'races' were not better subjects for inquiry than a myriad of individuals, and whether 'advanced races' could control their destinies by governmental, social, or perhaps even genetic organization. This concept—a marrying of the British science of evolution and the German concept of the organic state—powerfully affected contemporary thought: the language of 'race' became the common coin of reformers right across the political spectrum, from Rudyard Kipling, ostensibly the poet of the right, through J. A. Hobson and L. T. Hobhouse, the philosophers of the new liberals, to G. B. Shaw, regarded as the playwright of the left. The popular form of social Darwinism readily became a facile assumption of racial superiority, linked to imperialism, as the popular press reported the successes of the many small-scale colonial military expeditions. Popular reporting of these emphasized the importance of individual daring, character, and initiative, 'deeds that won the Empire', rather than the enormous technical disparity between a disciplined European army armed with rifles and from the 1890s the occasional machine-gun, and local forces relying on massed use of spears or, at best, sporadic musket fire.

Criticism of the liberal state in its classic Victorian form came from three chief political directions: from discontented Conservatives and Unionists who believed their political leadership was excessively hidebound by the canons of Peel–Gladstone fiscal policy, from Liberals who believed Liberalism must move on to meet new challenges, and from socialists who, at least at first glance, challenged the whole order of the state. Elements from each of these came together to demand 'national efficiency', a slogan intended to suggest a willingness to use government power to organize and legislate for an 'Imperial race' fit to meet the challenges of the world.

The free-trade state had always had its critics. The most influential of these in the second half of the nineteenth century was John Ruskin, art critic and social commentator. Politically impossible to categorize, Ruskin's powerful prose in works such as *Unto this Last* (1862) attacked the aesthetics of industrial society, but he offered no very systematic critique. His aesthetic criticisms were taken up by the Pre-Raphaelite Brotherhood, a group of painters, writers, and craftsmen who emphasized, especially through the writings and designs of William Morris, the values of pre-industrial England, a mythical land of craftsmen, contented peasants, and romance. From such influences sprang wide-ranging changes in design and architecture, epitomized by the 'English style' of domestic architecture of Norman Shaw and, at the turn of the century, Lutyens, which characterized the best of the building of the new suburbs. From Morris also sprang a socialist rhetoric of enduring potency: the image of a rural, self-sufficient, egalitarian society of sturdy yeomen. Morris did not confront industrialization, he by-passed it.

The aestheticism of the Pre-Raphaelites, and their general critique of middle-class morality, was given fresh impetus by the aesthetes of the 1880s and 1890s, the most notable of whom was the wit and playwright Oscar Wilde, ruined, like his fellow Irishman Parnell, by the public exposure of his sexual habits. Wilde's remarkable essay, 'The Soul of Man under Socialism', exemplified the links between aestheticism and individualist rather than collectivist socialism.

From 1884 these leanings towards socialism were supplemented by the London-based Fabian Society whose members included Sidney and Beatrice Webb, George Bernard Shaw, H. G. Wells, and, later, the young Ramsay MacDonald, all strong social evolutionists. The Fabians' criticism of the Liberal economic order was not so much that it was unjust, but that it was inefficient and wasteful: a centrally-planned economy and labour market, administered by an élite of trained professionals, would eliminate inefficiency, the trade cycle, and its by-products such as unemployment and poverty. It would attain this end gradually through legislation and not by revolution (hence the name Fabian, after the Roman general whose tactics the society emulated). Perhaps the chief contribution of the Fabians was to assist in the development of a fresh concept of 'progress' on the British left which in the 1880s was becoming limited in its horizons by the persistent wrangles over Home Rule. For the Fabians addressed themselves to the existing intelligentsia: they were not a popular movement. But popular discontent with the limitations of Gladstonian Liberalism was also developing; Keir Hardie, a coal-miner from the Ayrshire coalfield, represented the view that the increasingly unionized working class must have its own representatives in the House of Commons (where MPs were still not paid). Hardie, elected for West Ham in 1892, helped form the Scottish Parliamentary Labour Party in 1888 and, in 1893, founded the Independent Labour Party in Bradford. The ILP saw itself as a socialist party, but it had difficulty in establishing a popularly-supported organization. It shared with the Liberals an anti-imperialist rhetoric, supported 'Home Rule All Round', but called also for nationalization. H. M. Hyndman's Social Democratic Federation was more vigorous in its quasi-Marxist ideology, but gained very little popular foothold.

Old Liberalism, New Liberalism, Labourism, and Tariff Reform

All these movements were limited in their impact; the Liberals remained overwhelmingly the dominant party of the 'left' (the use of the word became common in British political discussion for the first time in the 1880s). None the less, the ideas being put forward, and the threat of their organizational success, concentrated Liberal minds. Liberals made their own contribution to the intellectual debates of the last two decades of the century. Always the party of land reform, their enthusiasm for it was rekindled by works such as the American Henry George's *Progress and Poverty* (1880). Posing the question, 'what *does* produce poverty amid advancing wealth?', George's answer was, crudely stated, the rents of the landed proprietor and the exclusion of workmen from free access to land, both rural and urban. The solution was a thoroughgoing and efficient land tax, known as 'the single tax'. The land campaign was a major theme of radicalism until the First World War, and beyond.

'Why do we sit and quietly behold degradation worse than that from which we have rescued women and children in mines and factories?' asked Arnold Toynbee, the liberal Christian historian and radical and, with T. H. Green, a great radical influence in the Oxford of the 1870s and early 1880s. Toynbee's followers (such as Canon Barnett, founder of Toynbee Hall in East London in 1884) encouraged, first, personal (often religious) commitment on the part of the intelligentsia to on-the-spot observation of working-class problems, and, second and later, an acceptance that voluntary effort would not be sufficient by itself to solve those problems. 'Advanced radicals' came to anticipate much greater government involvement in the economy, and much more 'positive liberalism' to see that each individual had the means by which he or she could make the most of his or her individual abilities. This was bound to cost money, and Liberals believed this money should be raised by increasing direct taxation, in particular death duties and a graduated income tax, to achieve a measure of redistribution at the same time as raising revenue. An important step in this direction was taken by the 1892–5 minority Liberal government which paid for increased social reform and naval expenditure by imposing for the first time an effective death duty. 'New

Liberalism', as this movement came to be called, was an attempt to justify the free-market system by making it work 'fairly'; it attempted a rationalization of capitalism, not its replacement. The movement, whose most effective author was J. A. Hobson, also a strong critic of 'immoral' imperialism, hoped to convert the Liberal Party to 'New Liberalism' and thus to allow the continuation of the Liberals as a broadly-based party, capable of continuing to assimilate and integrate the urban working class. This would avoid the German situation, where the working class had formed its own class-based Marxist party which rejected the legitimacy of the German State. This view was reinforced by political expediency on the Liberals' part. Following a series of adverse legal decisions which questioned their legal right to picket and their freedom from damages culminating in the famous Taff Vale case (1900–1), some trade unions, now in the late 1890s growing fast, joined with the ILP to form the Labour Representation Committee in 1900. The Liberals, split three ways by the Boer War, were at their weakest, and seemed to be able to offer the trade unionists, hitherto Liberal, little chance of redress. The secretary of the LRC, Ramsay MacDonald, negotiated an electoral agreement with the Liberals in February 1903, by which Liberal and Labour constituency parties would not split the progressive vote to let in a Unionist, but would reach local agreements by which a number of Labour candidates would have a good chance of being elected.

This accommodation between the two parties of the left showed the considerable area of agreement that existed between them: the Labour Party (as the LRC became in 1906) was part of the 'party of progress', at least for the time being, sharing many of its reforming aspirations, and its commitment to free trade.

The Unionists (as the coalition of Tories and Liberal-Unionists should be called after 1895 when Joseph Chamberlain and Lord Hartington, the Liberal-Unionist leaders, entered Salisbury's Cabinet) wished to conserve the British constitution as it then stood. But most of them also conserved its fiscal arrangements and remained free traders. Lord Salisbury gave no effective support to protection despite his large majority in both Houses. The imperialist faction within his party, however, increasingly came to see some form of imperial protection as essential. Their reasons for this were threefold. First, they believed that the growing success of the American and German economies was due to the protection of young industries, and that in the new era of technically sophisticated industry—chemicals, electricals, automobiles—Britain would lost out unless there was protection, a degree of planning, and much more co-operation between industry and education, all things that only government could supervise. Second, they believed that an Imperial Customs Union (analogous to the German *Zollverein* of the early nineteenth century) could integrate the empire's economy, Britain producing manufactured goods, the colonies raw materials. Third, they saw tariffs, including duties on food, as the only alternative to direct taxation to pay for the social reforms necessary to make the imperial race fit for the increasingly harsh competition between nations which they believed the future would bring. This programme was embodied in the Tariff Reform campaign launched by Joseph Chamberlain in 1903 while still Colonial Secretary, much to the embarrassment of the Prime Minister, Arthur Balfour, who had succeeded his uncle, Lord Salisbury, the previous year. Well financed, sophisticatedly organized and presented, Tariff Reform divided the Unionist Party (though the young Winston Churchill was one of the few MPs who actually left it). It was renounced by the electorate in a series of by-elections and then in the general election of 1906, when the Liberals together with 29 Labour MPs returned with a huge overall majority. England had turned from Home Rule in the 1880s and 1890s, but not from free trade. The Peel–Gladstone tradition of open markets and cheap food still carried great weight: 'the big loaf and the little loaf' was the Liberals' effective catch-phrase.

But although the 1906 Liberal success was the result mainly of negative factors—hostility to Tariff Reform, the dislike of Balfour's 1902 Education Act by nonconformists (their ranks swollen by a great religious revival), general criticism of the Unionists' handling of imperial affairs—the atmosphere had changed. There was much 'old Liberalism' (and 'old Toryism') still around, but the critiques of the Victorian liberal state made from the left, the right, and by Liberals themselves, bit deep.

The opening years of the twentieth century (there was much debate as to whether it began on 1 January 1900 or 1901) brought the widespread use by the better-off of its characteristic appliances, available in the 1890s but slow to find markets because of technical inadequacies—electric light in the houses, telephones, typewriters, gramophones, automobiles —and, soon, wireless and aeroplanes. The first building in the world specially designed as a cinema was opened in Colne, Lancashire, in 1907. Quite suddenly, the Victorian years and their preoccupations began to seem worlds away. The deaths of the three most notable public figures of those years—Gladstone in 1898, Victoria herself in 1901, Salisbury in 1903—emphasized the change.

Edwardian Years: a Crisis of the State Contained

Reappraisals of the nineteenth-century state were reinforced by a series of social enquiries in the 1890s and early 1900s into the working of the labour market and into social conditions— investigations such as Charles Booth's *Life and Labour of the People in London* (which appeared in four series of thirty-three volumes in all, 1889–1903) and Seebohm Rowntree's *Poverty: a study of town life* (1901). Booth and Rowntree for the first time attempted to define 'poverty' as a social phenomenon (as opposed to the Poor Law's definition of pauperism which was a legal category). Rowntree found over 27 per cent of the population of York living in what he called 'primary or secondary poverty'. Standards of living might have risen for employed working people since the 1880s, but a significant proportion of the population was shown still to live in 'poverty' (a relative term) and on the brink of economic disaster. This contrasted markedly with the flamboyant 'plutocratic' living, noted earlier, of some members of the court and aristocracy.

Almost 30 per cent living in poverty was shocking, and it shocked contemporaries. But it also meant that 70 per cent were living in relative affluence, a proportion inconceivable in the days of the 'iron law of wages' of the mid-century. In the 1860s, Gladstone as Chancellor had admitted that the economy necessarily functioned with an 'enormous mass of paupers', and Victorians had been aware, in an ill-defined and helpless way, of the waste and suffering around them. Matthew Arnold's *Culture and Anarchy* (1869) described London's East End as containing 'those vast, miserable, unmanageable masses of sunken people'. Their reactions to it had been consequently local and personal, in the form of personal, charitable endeavour to alleviate the lot of those actually known to them or of particular categories of the so-called 'deserving poor', for example, distressed gentlefolk. Now, at the turn of the century, systematic investigation not only raised alarm that an 'imperial race' could be so impoverished, but, by providing figures, suggested manageability and means of redress: until the scale of the problem was known, it could not be tackled. 'While the problem of 1834 was the problem of pauperism, the problem of 1893 is the problem of poverty' remarked Alfred Marshall, the leading free-trade economist; he implied that the problem of poverty had become both definable and solvable.

The Liberal governments of 1905–14, especially after Asquith became Prime Minister in 1908 on Campbell-Bannerman's death, made a considerable attempt to begin to come to terms with these questions. Free school meals (1907), old age pensions (a scheme drawn up in 1908 by Asquith before becoming Prime Minister, though seen through the Commons by David Lloyd George, his successor as Chancellor of the Exchequer); the Development Act (1909) anticipating Keynesian deficit financing; Winston Churchill's labour exchanges (1909); and Lloyd George's National Insurance Bill (1911) giving compulsory insurance to certain workers for benefits in times of sickness and unemployment, paid for by the State, the employer, and the employee—these and a host of smaller measures constituted the first legislative milestones of the modern welfare state. They were based on the rejection of the Victorian principle that individual probity and diligence would ensure modest prosperity: the reforms accepted that capitalism was wasteful, inefficient, and punishing to individuals regardless of personal merit, and that 'voluntaryism' was not enough. But they were none the less the reforms of free-traders who believed that marginal adjustments to the system could phase out the injustices of capitalism and make it 'fair'.

These reforms were expensive but based on a wide measure of consensus; it was the raising of revenue to pay for them which caused particular controversy, a controversy compounded by the need to raise large sums to pay for a fleet of 'Dreadnought' ships to match German naval expansion. The Tariff Reformers advocated protective indirect taxes to raise such revenues: the Liberals legislated for expanded direct taxes. Lloyd George's budget of 1909 brought a long-festering issue to a head by introducing a 'super-tax' on the incomes of the very rich and an attempt at an effective tax on land. Balfour and the Unionists used the House of Lords to throw out the budget.

This was the culmination of increasing use of the Lords to frustrate Liberal legislation: the Home Rule Bill of 1893 and a series of measures in 1906–8 had been either mutilated or destroyed. The rejection of the budget, traditionally the prerogative of the Commons, struck at a central tenet of British representative government. The Unionists argued that the conventional exemption of financial legislation meant that Liberals were using it to 'tack' on what was really social legislation—but all taxation was, and always had been, ultimately social in its consequences. Two general elections in 1910 left the Liberals dependent on Labour and Irish support, but none the less with a clear majority against the Lords: the Unionist leadership—though not all its followers—eventually conceded the point and the Parliament Act of 1911 limited the Lords' veto to two years.

This great institutional battle had begun with a basic question about social organization: where would the extra tax burden fall—on the rich through the super-tax or on the poor through food taxes? Its progress raised another, about constitutional organization. For the Liberals, as required by their Irish supporters, now introduced the third Home Rule Bill which, together with disestablishment of the Anglican Church in Wales, became law under the provisions of the Parliament Act in 1914, though suspended in practice for the duration of the war.

The Unionists reluctantly swallowed the budget, but Home Rule they would not stomach. With implicit encouragement from their new leader, Andrew Bonar Law (who replaced Balfour in 1911), they took literally the slogan coined by Lord Randolph Churchill in 1886: 'Ulster will fight and Ulster will be right.' Guns, many of them German, were shipped to Northern Ireland. There was doubt about the loyalty of the army to the State. Three times denied possession of power by the electorate of the United Kingdom as a whole, the Unionists brought Ireland to the edge of civil war in 1914 despite substantial Liberal concessions on the Ulster question, which might have been introduced rather earlier. The outbreak of the First World War prevented posterity from knowing whether the Unionists would have gone over that edge.

Edwardian Britain was thus a turbulent time for politics and politicians. The resurgence of Liberalism and the Liberals' willingness to come to terms with many problems long delayed or frustrated was a painful business for the Unionists, who continue to regard themselves, in or out of power, as the natural rulers of the nation.

But if an old élite's decline caused the greatest trouble, new, rising forces were also very active. The movement for women's suffrage went back to J. S. Mill's attempt to amend the 1867

Reform Bill to give women the vote. Some progress was made, for some women gained the vote for local elections, and for the synod of the Church of England, and could stand as candidates for local councils, school boards, and the poor law board. But the marginal public role given to middle-class women in the 1870s and 1880s—helping the priest, the doctor, or the MP; being secretary to the charity whose chairman was almost always a man; taking university examinations but not degrees—was no longer enough. Exclusion from voting for elections of the imperial Parliament exemplified what had come to be seen as deprivation; the campaign for women's votes was a campaign for a new concept of citizenship. Mrs Fawcett's National Union of Women's Suffrage Societies, uniting in 1897 a number of well-established organizations, was a broadly-based movement of impeccably liberal credentials which made considerable headway. It was, however, outflanked and outshone by the Pankhursts' Women's Social and Political Union (1903). The WSPU increasingly advocated violence against both property and individual politicians, as well as inflicting through imprisonment and hunger strikes considerable hardship and even occasionally death upon its members. Whether the WSPU helped or hindered the cause is hard to say: on the one hand, it dramatized it, on the other, its support for violence alienated many potential supporters among MPs and in particular Asquith, the Prime Minister, and made its legislative success less likely. Despite committed support within the Liberal and Labour Parties, and from a few Unionists, no legislation had been passed by 1914.

The Edwardian years also saw a very considerable expansion of the trade union movement, from 2.0 million members in 1901 to 4.1 million in 1913. In the years after 1908, price inflation and stationary wages encouraged this burgeoning movement to exert its strength; and there was a series of major strikes in 1910–12, culminating in the first general railway strike in 1911, which Lloyd George, as Chancellor, defused—also something of a precedent. Since Labour Party membership could only be held through being a trade union member, and since most trade unions came to be affiliated to the Labour Party (the affiliation in 1909 of the coal-miners, the chief union still hitherto supporting the Liberals, was a particular triumph), the Labour Party grew considerably in strength. A wide network of constituency parties was established with a ferment of ideological discussion, much of it necessarily Utopian in character (much of it inspired by William Morris), for the means of implementation was as yet very limited. The party had a secure base in the Commons, but of a limited size, and considerably dependent on its pact with the Liberals which brought it some thirty seats at the 1906 election. Its limited success at elections was not surprising, given that in the sort of industrial seats in which it would expect to succeed, about 60 per cent of adult men were not enfranchised. As yet, the party in the Commons saw itself largely as a pressure group for trade union interests, successfully amending the original Liberal bill so as to prevent the legal incorporation of the unions through the 1906 Trade Disputes Act, the consequence of the Taff Vale case. The Labour Party also intervened on social questions and on foreign policy. This slow progress at Westminster led some trade unionists (notably some of the Welsh miners) to turn to syndicalism, that is, 'direct action' by trade unions to promote workers' control, circumventing MPs, Parliament, and the mechanisms of representative government.

The Labour Party's existence and success, closely linked to the expansion and difficulties of trade unionism, reflected a social, as much as an intellectual, difference from the Liberals. The solidarity of the Labour movement was based on cultural and social affinities, the shared experiences of working people in work and leisure, as much as any articulated perception of themselves as a separate class. Working people did not feel themselves to be alienated from the propertied classes, but they did feel themselves to be different. The Liberals reinforced this by their failure to adopt working men as candidates: however broad the agreement on policy matters, the middle-class members of the Liberal Associations—the people who called the tune in the constituencies—would not adopt as candidates men whom they would expect to enter their houses by the servants' door.

'Your English summer's done'

The refurbished Liberalism of the Edwardian years thus faced many difficulties. Legislatively, it met these dynamically and imaginatively with the first of the two great reforming governments of the century. It successfully contained and in large measure resolved the crisis over fiscal policy, welfare policy, socialism, and militarism which had brought many Continental nations to a political impasse by 1914 (though Ireland remained potentially an exception to this). It was not domestic divisions which were to bring Liberal governments in Britain to an end, but foreign affairs. We noted earlier the ambivalent consequences of the *Entente* policy pursued by Lord Lansdowne, Balfour's Foreign Secretary, and between 1905 and 1914 by Sir Edward Grey for the Liberals. Britain was committed implicitly and emotionally, but not in terms spelt out, to the French–Russian side of the European equation. Secret military conversations after 1905 between the British and the French increased this commitment. Although the greatest imperial power, Britain could bring little direct influence to bear on Continental affairs. R. B. Haldane's army reforms developed an Expeditionary Force intended for Europe, but, though efficient, it was tiny compared to the vast, conscript armies of the Continental powers. Indeed, the Germans simply discounted it, to their cost. As the concept of the 'Concert of Europe' gave way to overtly nationalistic self-assertion, the British contribution waned. Though personally strongly anti-German, Grey continued to avoid formal alliances, but by 1910 it was clear that Germany would be Britain's adversary, if she were to have one. In a series of incidents in North Africa, the Balkans, and Turkey, and in the continuing escalation of the navy building programme (despite British attempts, especially in 1911–12, to negotiate a limitation agreement) Anglo-German hostility became confirmed. It began to take on a cultural as well as a diplomatic and military aspect. The respect mixed with concern characteristic of British views of German achievements in the 1890s began to change to alarm and fear.

When events in the Balkans and Central Europe in June and July 1914 led rapidly to war, as Germany estimated that the moment for her bid for mastery had come, the British could bring little influence to bear. Britain had less to gain from war than any of the other major European powers except perhaps Russia. Whether the Liberal Cabinet would have entered the war at all had the Germans not invaded Belgium is open to doubt. But the Germans ignored both the traditional British concern for the strategic importance of the Low Countries, and the implications of guarantee of Belgian independence which they as well as the British had signed in 1870 to last during the Franco-Prussian War. The attack on Belgium decided the matter, and Asquith led his Cabinet into war with only two resignations—John Morley and John Burns. He did so with a heavy heart: the blithe spirit which infused the enthusiastic rush to the colours to join the war that was to be 'over by Christmas' was not shared by Britain's political leadership.

Britain was remarkably unprepared psychologically and, on the whole, physically for a Continental land war. War on land, even in the Crimea and South Africa, had been seen as a marginal matter, to be fought by professionals and a few volunteers. Military values were influential amongst the aristocracy and gentry and increasingly in the public schools, but elsewhere made little impact. Attempts by groups on the right to militarize society—from the Militia of the 1850s through the Riflemen and the Volunteers, to Lord Roberts's National Service League in the 1900s—had conspicuously failed. 'Trafalgar Day' was the annual martial celebration, reflecting the essentially naval and defensive cast of the public mind—the 'blue water' policy, as it was called. Except in certain rural areas, 'to go for a sodger', 'to take the King's shilling', had for ordinary people been an act of desperation in a time of unemployment or personal catastrophe. The British public liked bands and bright uniforms because they were entertainments, the exact opposite of harbingers of war. Pomp and domesticity was the British style. Government contracts for guns and ships were by the Edwardian years considerable in value and an important part of the economy of the northeast of England, but, in general, military matters seldom impinged on the thinking of government and society. Certainly, they had not penetrated the very fabric of the political, social, and economic order as they had in virtually every Continental state. The first industrial nation had offered the world a remarkable public experiment in liberal, capitalist democracy whose success was premised upon free trade and world peace. Tuesday, 4 August 1914 brought that experiment to an abrupt halt.

There's a whisper down the field where the year has shot her yield,
And the ricks stand grey to the sun,
Singing:—'Over then, come over, for the bee has quit the clover,
And your English summer's done.'

Rudyard Kipling, 'The Long Trail'

2. The Twentieth Century
(1914–1987)

KENNETH O. MORGAN

The First World War

AT the Lord Mayor of London's annual banquet at the Mansion House on 17 July 1914, the Chancellor of the Exchequer, David Lloyd George, issued stern warnings about the ominous condition of British society. At home, the 'triple alliance' of miners, railwaymen, and transport workers was threatening a mass united strike to back up the railwaymen's claim for union recognition and a 48-hour week. Alongside this prospect of nation-wide industrial paralysis, there was across the Irish Sea a state of near civil war in Ireland, with 200,000 or more men under arms in Protestant Ulster and the Catholic south, and the likelihood of the age-long saga of Irish nationalism being brought to a grim and bloody resolution. Abroad, there were nationalist troubles in India and in Egypt. Nearer home in south-east Europe, the ethnic nationalities of the Balkans were in renewed turmoil following the assassination of the Austrian Archduke, Franz Ferdinand, at Sarajevo in Bosnia on 28 June.

On the eve of world war, therefore, Britain seemed to present a classic picture of a civilized liberal democracy on the verge of dissolution, racked by tensions and strains with which its sanctions and institutions were unable to cope. And yet, as so often in the past, once the supreme crisis of war erupted, these elements of conflict subsided with remarkable speed. An underlying mood of united purpose gripped the nation. The first few weeks of hostilities, after Britain declared war on 4 August, were, inevitably, a time of some panic. Only dramatic measures by the Treasury and the Bank of England preserved the national currency and credit. Manufacturing and commerce tried desperately to adjust to the challenges of war against the background of an ethic that proclaimed that it was 'business as usual'. The early experiences of actual fighting were almost disastrous as the British Expeditionary Force, cobbled together in much haste and dispatched to Flanders and France, met with a severe reverse at Ypres, and had to retreat from Mons, in disarray and suffering heavy losses. Reduced to only three corps in strength, its fighting force was gravely diminished almost from the start. Only a stern resistance by the French forces on the river Marne prevented a rapid German advance on Paris and an early victory for Germany and its Austrian allies.

After the initial disasters, however, the nation and its leaders settled down for a long war. Vital domestic issues such as Irish home rule were suspended for the duration of hostilities. The political parties declared an indefinite truce. The industrial disturbances of the summer of 1914 petered out, with the TUC out-doing the employers in voicing the conventional patriotism of the time. A curious kind of calm descended, founded on a broad—though very far from universal—consensus about the justice of the war. The one element required to make it acceptable to a liberal society was some kind of broad, humane justification to explain what the war was really about. This was provided by Lloyd George, once a bitter opponent of the Boer War in South Africa in 1899, and for many years the most outspokenly left-wing member of the Asquith Liberal government. Lloyd George remained suspiciously silent during the early weeks. But in an eloquent address to a massed audience of his Welsh fellow-countrymen at the Queen's Hall, London, on 19 September 1914, he committed himself without reserve to a fight to the finish. He occupied, or claimed to occupy, the highest moral ground. It was, he declared, a war on behalf of liberal principles, a crusade on behalf of the 'little five-foot-five nations', like Belgium, flagrantly invaded by the Germans, or Serbia and Montenegro, now threatened by Austria-Hungary. It was not surprising that a claim that the war was a holy cause, backed up not only by the leaders of all the Christian churches but by all the Liberal pantheon of heroes from Fox to Gladstone, met with instant response, not least in the smaller nations of Scotland and Wales within Britain itself.

This broad consensus about the rightness of the war was not fundamentally eroded over the next four terrible years. Of course, it went through many changes, especially after the unpopular decision to impose conscription for the armed services was instituted in May 1916. Eventually, by 1917, sheer war-weariness was taking its toll, quite apart from other factors such as the growing militancy from organized labour and the Messianic appeal of the Bolshevik revolution in Russia. Of course, too, this consensus was sustained by subtle or crude manipulation of the news services, censorship of the press, government-sponsored legends of atrocities allegedly committed by 'the Huns'. There was much persecution of radical or anti-war critics. In spite of government pressures, bodies such as the Christian pacifist 'No-Conscription Fellowship' and the Union of Democratic Control (which sought a negotiated peace) were by 1917 making some impact on public opinion. Lord Lansdowne's appeal for peace (29 November 1917) caused a great stir. Nevertheless, the available evidence for the war years suggests that the broad mass of the population retained its faith that the war was just and necessary, and that it must be fought until the total surrender of the German enemy, whatever the cost. Recruitment to the armed services from volunteers was heavy and enthusiastic: indeed voluntary recruitment proved more successful in swelling the ranks of the army in France in 1914–16 than was the compulsory method of conscription thereafter. The long years of military and naval conflict that dragged on from the initial stalemate on the western front in the autumn of 1914, until the final Allied breakthrough in August–September 1918 were accepted with resignation and a kind of grim endurance.

The psychological and moral impact of those appalling years sank deep into the memory and the outlook of the British people. They profoundly coloured the literary sensibilities of a whole generation. They helped shape responses to the threat of foreign war for twenty years after the Great War came to an end. The war on the western front took the unfamiliar form of a prolonged slogging match between heavily-defended forces on either side, dug into slit trenches, and unable to exploit the new techniques of mobile striking power so dramatically tested in the Franco-Prussian war of 1870. For almost four years, the war in France showed little movement. There were occasional British attempts to seize the initiative. Always they ended in huge casualties on a scale scarcely comprehensible to a nation which lived on the luxurious memories of a century of almost unbroken peace. The British offensive at Loos was beaten back in September 1915. More damaging still, in June 1916 a new British advance on the Somme proved a calamitous failure with 60,000 men falling on the first day. British casualties here alone amounted to 420,000. The most terrible of these experiences came at Passchendaele in August–September 1917, when over 300,000 British troops were recorded as dead or wounded, many of them drowned in the mud of Flanders amidst torrential rain. Both the cavalry and mechanical inventions such as the 'tanks' made no impact in so immobile a campaign. The new fighter aircraft had little effect. As on other occasions, the class divide that cut off commanding officers from the rank-and-file infantrymen and hindered communication between them was fatal throughout. In effect, the British ceased to be a viable offensive force for the next few months. March and April 1918 saw the British army desperately striving to ward off a new German advance in the Amiens sector. Nor until the ultimate dramatic breakthrough by Haig that August did the war show signs of coming to a resolution. Meanwhile attempts, advocated by Lloyd George and Churchill amongst others, to circumvent the stalemate on the western front by a more peripheral 'eastern' strategy also led to successive débâcles. The Dardanelles expedition in the summer of 1915 was a colossal exercise in military mismanagement and led to further huge losses; so did the expedition to Salonika a year later. The Dardanelles in particular did immense harm to Churchill's reputation as a rational politician, from which he took years to recover. Even on the high seas, Britain's traditional area of supremacy, the one major battle, the encounter off Jutland in June 1916, was at best a draw between the British and German high fleets. The British Grand Fleet lost three battle cruisers, three other cruisers, and eight destroyers in an ill-conducted engagement.

Later anti-war propaganda depicted an angry populace displaying fierce hostility towards the military and naval commanders responsible for this terrible catalogue of disaster in almost every theatre. 'War poets' such as Wilfred Owen and Isaac Rosenberg (who fell in battle) and Siegfried Sassoon and Robert Graves (who survived), stirred particularly by the carnage of Passchendaele, all encouraged the view that a mass renunciation took place of the very idea of war itself, of the carnage that could result in half an entire generation of young men being wiped out. The bare statistics of the war—750,000 killed, another 2,500,000 wounded, many permanently disabled—reinforced this belief in a mass rejection of militarism. That was not, however, how it appeared to most people at the time, even if it should have done so. While the British commander-in-chief on the western front, Sir John French, was indeed removed from command at the end of 1915, his successor, Sir Douglas Haig, a grim, taciturn Lowland Scot, steadily built up a massive public reputation for courage and integrity, a reputation matched by Sir Edwin Lutyens's towering war memorial to commemorate the British dead at Thiepval. Other naval and military leaders, such as Admiral Beatty and General Allenby (who conducted a brilliant campaign from Egypt, through Palestine into Syria in 1917–18, to eliminate the Turks as significant allies for the Germans) became almost popular heroes. The trenches became the symbol of stern, but inescapable, resolution. Bruce Bairnsfather's famous cartoon of 'Old Bill', urging his comrade that if he knew of 'a better 'ole' he should go to it, symbolized a popular mood of almost humorous tolerance of the terrors of trench warfare. When, after desperate military crises and with the immense military and financial aid of the United States, the British and French armies forced their way through the German lines to reach the borders of Germany itself by the time of the armistice on 11 November 1918, mass enthusiasm for the war appeared at its zenith. Britain seemed in danger of inventing a new military cult unknown in these islands since the days of Marlborough.

A major factor in the widespread popularity of the war—and also in its subsequent bitter unpopularity—was the involvement of the whole population and the entire social and economic fabric in total war. After a leisurely start, in 1915–16 the war brought about a massive industrial and social transformation; it erected a leviathan of state power and collectivist control without precedent. The forces of production and distribution in industry and agriculture were all harnessed to fuel the needs of a mighty war machine. The model was set by the new Ministry of Munitions of which Lloyd George assumed control in May 1915. Created to deal with bottle-necks in the supply of arms and ammunition, the Ministry became the engine of a massive central machine which invigorated the entire industrial structure through its 'men of push and go'. It achieved an immense impact as well on such different areas as social welfare, housing policy, and the status of women. The coal mines, the railways, merchant and other shipping were all taken under state control. The old pre-war shibboleths of *laissez-faire*, including the hallowed principle of free trade itself, were bypassed or ignored. Equally, the traditional system of industrial relations was wrenched into totally new patterns. The Treasury Agreement of March 1915, negotiated between the government and the trade unions (except for the miners), forbade strikes but also guaranteed collective bargaining and, indirectly, a new access to government for trade union leaders. The Treasury Agreement certainly did not achieve its aim of universal industrial peace during the war years. There were major disputes in the coal industry, notably a successful official strike by the South Wales Miners in July 1915. The work of the Ministry of Munitions in trying to 'dilute' the work-force by introducing unskilled workers (especially women) into engineering factories, and in trying to control the movements of labour in the armaments industry brought much trouble, notably on Clydeside. The unofficial activities of shop stewards in Scotland and also in Sheffield in 1916–17 remind us that the consensus of the war years was a shallow one and very far from unanimous. Nevertheless, the war did ensure a continuing corporate status for the unions—and also for employers, newly combined in the Federation of British Industry. A new organic, planned system of industrial relations appeared to be possible. It was significant that powerful businessmen such as Sir Eric Geddes and Sir Joseph Maclay, Lord Devonport and Lord Rhondda, appeared in key departments of central government. This symbolized the transformation in the relationship of industrial and political leadership that was taking place. Edward VII's Liberal England was being turned into a corporate state, almost what a later generation would term 'Great Britain Limited'.

Over a vast range of social and cultural activities, the collective impact of the Great War was profound indeed. Left-wing opponents of the war such as Ramsay MacDonald of the Labour Party noted ironically that the imperatives of war were achieving far more for social reform than had all the campaigns of the trade unions and of progressive humanitarians in half a century past. New vistas of governmental activity were being opened up. Fresh layers were being added to the techno-cratic, professional, and civil service élite that had governed Britain in the years of peace. The administrative and managerial class expanded massively. Social reformers such as William Beveridge or Seebohm Rowntree, even the socialist Beatrice Webb, became influential and even honoured figures in the recesses of central government, especially after Lloyd George succeeded Asquith as Prime Minister in December 1916. Wages went up; working conditions improved. The 1917 Corn Production Act revitalized British agriculture and gave a fresh lease of life to tenant farmers and their labourers. Attention was also paid to technical and other education, notably through H. A. L. Fisher's Act of 1918 which made free elementary education general and sought to create a ladder of opportunity from the elementary to the secondary and higher levels of education. Governmental inquiries, one of them headed by as conservative a figure as Lord Salisbury, opened up new vistas for state housing schemes, an area almost totally neglected by the New Liberalism before 1914. The principle was laid down for a system of subsidized local-authority houses, to provide the hundreds of thousands of working-class dwellings for rent that were required, and to remove the blight of slums in city centres and older industrial areas. Concern was voiced, too, for public health. The supreme irony was that a war which brought the loss of human life on such a colossal scale also saw the preservation of life at home through improved medical arrangements, better conditions for children and old people and nursing mothers, and such innovations as the Medical Research Council. By the end of 1918, the government was committed to the idea of a new Ministry of Health to co-ordinate the services for health and national insurance, and to take over the duties of the Local Government Board.

One important element of British society above all other gained from the wartime experience—indeed for them (a majority of the population, in fact) this was an era of emancipation. Women in Britain were supreme beneficiaries of the war years. Thousands of them served at the front, often in medical field hospitals. The spectacle of Nurse Edith Cavell martyred by the Germans for assisting in the escape of British and French prisoners of war in Belgium added powerfully to the public esteem of women in general. At home, suffragette leaders such as Mrs Pankhurst and her elder daughter Christabel (though not her socialist younger daughter, Sylvia) aided in recruiting campaigns for the government. More widely, women found vast new opportunities in clerical and administrative work, in munitions and other engineering factories, and in many other unfamiliar tasks previously reserved for men only. The very dissolution wrought by total war exerted powerful pressures in eroding the sex barriers which had restricted British women over the decades. It was hardly possible to argue now that women were incapable of exercising the rights of citizenship to the full; in the 1918 Representation of the People Act, therefore, women aged 30 and over were given the vote. It was almost anti-climactic. A long, bitter saga of persecution and prejudice ended with a whimper. Here as elsewhere, by emphasizing the positive, progressive consequences of the war, with the full panoply of 'reconstruction' (ill-defined) which was supposed to be launched when peace returned, the government contrived, perhaps unintentionally, to extend and fortify the consensus of the time.

For British politics, the Great War produced massive and tumultuous changes. At the outbreak of war, the House of Commons was still largely dominated by the Gilbertian rivalry of Liberals and Conservatives (or Unionists). However, for the Liberal Party the war brought disaster. Partly this was because of the serious inroads into individual and civil liberties that war entailed. Partly it was due to a deep-seated ambiguity about the very merits of the war that many Liberals harboured. The turning of Asquith's Liberal administration into a three-party coalition in May 1915 marked a new stage in the downfall of Liberalism. Thereafter, Asquith's own apparently lethargic and fumbling leadership was accompanied by severe internal party divisions over the fundamental issue of military conscription.

Lloyd George and Churchill both endorsed conscription as the symbol of whole-hearted commitment to 'a fight to the finish'. More traditional Liberals such as Simon and McKenna were hesitant. Asquith himself dithered unhappily. In the end, conscription came for all adult males aged between eighteen and forty-five, but criticism of Asquith and the Liberal ethic generally continued to mount.

In December 1916 the final crisis came. There had been complaints for months over government failures, not only in the field, but also over the inability to resolve the Irish question and to settle labour disputes at home. Between 1 and 9 December 1916 there followed political manœuvres of Byzantine complexity over which historians continue to dispute like so many medieval schoolmen. Lloyd George joined with two leading Unionists, Bonar Law and the Irishman, Sir Edward Carson, in proposing to Asquith a new supreme War Committee to run the war. After days of uncertainty, Asquith refused. Lloyd George then resigned and, in a crucial trial of strength between 4 and 9 December, emerged as Prime Minister of something like an all-party coalition. It included not only all the Unionists but also (by a very narrow majority on the National Executive) the Labour Party as well, in addition to roughly half the Liberals in the House of Commons. Henceforth, between December 1916 and November 1918, Lloyd George built himself up into a semi-presidential position of near-impregnability. He was the Prime Minister of a supreme War Cabinet, backed up by a new Cabinet office and a 'garden suburb' or kitchen cabinet of private secretaries. Beneath this apex extended a mighty machine of centralized power. Lloyd George's triumph helped to win the war—but for his own Liberal Party it meant a débâcle. The party remained split, weakened at the grass roots, ineffective and divided in Parliament, shorn of much of its morale and impetus in the press and in intellectual circles. The New Liberalism, which had animated so much social reform before 1914, just spluttered out. When the war ended in November 1918, the Liberals were a divided, much weakened rump, a supreme casualty of total war.

Their place was taken, quite unexpectedly, by the Labour Party. This party had also been much divided by the outbreak of war. In contrast to the patriotism of trade union leaders, Ramsay MacDonald and many on the socialist left had been opponents of entering the war. MacDonald had to resign his leadership of the parliamentary Labour Party in consequence. Issues during the war such as the impact of conscription (military and possible industrial), and the decision over whether or not to serve under Lloyd George also plagued the Labour Party. Nevertheless, the long-term consequences of the war for the party were wholly beneficial. The trade unions on which Labour depended were much strengthened by the war experience. Their membership roughly doubled to reach over eight million by the start of 1919. The party was also given new stimulus by the revolution in Russia, and by the wider anti-war radicalism in the last two years of the war. In effect, Labour was serving in government and acting as the formal opposition at one and the same time. It was ideally placed to exploit the internal difficulties of the Liberals. Finally, the 1918 franchise reforms extended the electorate from about 8 million to over 21 million. This meant a huge increase in the working-class vote and an encouragement of the tendency to polarize politics on grounds of class. The 1918 party constitution gave the party a new socialist commitment and, more important, a reorganized structure in the constituencies and in Head Office, dominated throughout by the trade unions. The advance of Labour was a powerful political consequence of the war, though quite unforeseen at the time.

The real beneficiaries were the Conservatives. The war encouraged a process by which they became the natural majority party. Apart from being united by the call by war, as the patriots they claimed to be, after being divided over tariffs and other questions before 1914, the Conservatives became

increasingly dominated by business and manufacturing interests. They were now largely urban or suburban in their base,
not a party of squires. At the end of the war, with new
business-orientated figures such as Stanley Baldwin and Neville
Chamberlain coming through, the Conservatives were poised,
like the Labour Party, to destroy the Edwardian political
system. When the war ended on 11 November 1918, Lloyd
George assumed total command. His rump of Coalition Liberals
were in electoral alliance with the Conservatives, in opposition
to the 'pacifists' of the anti-government Liberals and the
'Bolsheviks' of the Labour Party. A new era of right-wing
domination was in the making.

Externally, the war years encouraged further changes. It was,
in all senses, a profoundly imperial war, fought for empire as
well as for king and country. Much was owed to military and
other assistance from Australia, New Zealand, Canada, South
Africa, and India. Anzac Day (with memories of Suvla Bay,
Gallipoli) became a tragic, symbolic event in the Australian
calendar. In 1917 Lloyd George actually convened an Imperial
War Cabinet of Prime Ministers to assist the Cabinet of the
mother country. A powerful empire statesman like Smuts of
South Africa was even called upon to participate in the
deliberations of the British Cabinet. In commerce, imperial
preference was becoming a reality. The imperial mystique was a
powerful one at this time. The main architect of the day, Edwin
Lutyens, had been in his younger days a disciple of the arts and
crafts movement inspired by William Morris. Now he and
Herbert Baker were turning their talents to pomp and circumstance by rebuilding the city of Delhi. It was to be dominated
by a massive Viceroy's residence and Secretariat buildings as
symbols of classical authority. During the war years, the imperial idea was taken further than ever before. Indeed, the secret
treaties of the war years ensured that at the peace the mandate
system or other stratagems would leave Britain with an
imperial domain larger than ever, with vast new territories in
the Middle East and up from the Persian Gulf. Buoyed up by

the eccentric operations of individualists such as 'Lawrence of Arabia' and fired by the heady prospects of vast oil riches in Mesopotamia and elsewhere in the Middle East, the bounds of the British Empire extended ever wider.

Yet in reality it was all becoming increasingly impractical to maintain. Long before 1914, the financial and military constraints upon an effective imperial policy were becoming clear, especially in India with its growing Congress movement. There was something else now—new and increasingly effective nationalist uprisings against British rule. Unlike Wales, which was almost mindlessly patriotic with Lloyd George at the helm, Ireland offered a disturbing spectacle of colonial revolt. The Easter rising of April 1916, conducted by a few republicans and Sinn Fein partisans, seemed to be a fiasco. But, aided by the brutal reaction of Asquith's government, by mid-1918 Sinn Fein and its republican creed had won over almost all the twenty-six southern Irish counties. A veteran home ruler such as John Dillon was being swept aside by new nationalist radicals like Michael Collins and Eamon de Valera. By the end of the war, southern Ireland was virtually under martial law, resistant to conscription, in a state of near rebellion against the Crown and the Protestant ascendancy, or what was left of it. The long march of Irish nationalism, constitutional and largely peaceful in the decades from O'Connell to Parnell and Redmond, seemed on the verge of producing a new and violent explosion. One clear moral of the war years, therefore, was that the political and social consensus, fragile enough for Clydeside and the Welsh mining valleys, did not extend at all to southern Ireland. With the powerful thrust of Irish republicanism, a new kind of nationalist revolt against the constraints of imperial rule was well under way. Indians and Egyptians, among others, were likely to pay careful heed. The war left a legacy of a more integrated but also a more isolated Britain, whose grandiose imperial role was already being swamped by wider transformations in the post-war world.

The Twenties

When peace returned, it seemed that little had changed. The continuity between war and peace was confirmed by Lloyd George's overwhelming electoral triumph at the 'coupon election' of December 1918, a ratification of the patriotism and unity of the war years. The Prime Minister was acclaimed, almost universally, as 'the man who won the war', the most dominant political leader since Cromwell. The electoral verdict was indeed an overpowering one. The supporters of the coalition government numbered no less than 526 (of whom 136 were Liberals and almost all the rest Unionist), against a mere 57 Labour MPs and 26 Independent Liberals. The results were not so conclusive under closer examination. The Labour Party's tally of 57 MPs concealed the fact that the party had polled two and a half million votes, and was on the verge of a massive electoral breakthrough. In Ireland, Sinn Fein captured 73 seats out of 81 in the south; its representatives withdrew from Westminster and set up their own unofficial parliament or 'Dáil' in Dublin. Even so, the mandate on behalf of the Prime Minister and his wartime associates seemed quite irrefutable. The election seemed to confirm, too, that socio-economic normality in many respects was being rapidly restored. Many of the wartime controls and the apparatus of state collectivism disappeared as if they had never been. Major industries were returned to private hands—the railways, shipping, even the coal mines whose owners were perhaps the most hated group in the entire capitalist world. The government also began a consistent financial policy to ensure an eventual return to the gold standard; this would entail a deflationary approach, with a steady contraction of the note issue expanded so rapidly during the war. The City of London, the class system, private capitalism appeared destined to continue their unchallenged reign. To indicate that this was capitalism with a human face, the government also began with a flurry of reforming activity in

1919–20. Indeed, Lloyd George had campaigned far more vigorously at the election as a social reformer anxious to build a 'land fit for heroes', than as a chauvinist determined to hang the Kaiser or 'squeeze Germany till the pips squeaked'. So there followed a vigorous, if short-lived, programme to extend health and educational services, to raise pensions, and spread universal unemployment insurance. Most spectacular of all was the subsidized housing programme launched by the Liberal minister, Dr Christopher Addison, which, with reluctant treasury support, achieved a total of over 200,000 publicly-built houses in the 1919–22 period, a limited but valuable start in dealing with one of the major social scandals in the land.

But it soon became disturbingly clear that life was not normal and that the comforting framework of pre-1914 could not easily be restored. There were new and disruptive economic problems that resulted from the loss of foreign markets and the sale of overseas investments to pay for the war. The most ominous aspect of this, on which newspaper headlines focused attention, was the huge increase in the national debt. The unredeeemed capital of the debt stood at £706 million in 1914. Six years later it had soared to £7,875 millions. This resulted in a passionate cry for 'economy', the ending of 'waste' in public expenditure, and a return to a balanced budget and a firm currency after the rapid inflation of 1918–19. Politically, too, things were very far from normal. Lloyd George's coalition had come to power in unhappy circumstances, with a background of conspiracy surrounding the calling of the 1918 'coupon' general election. Its moral title to power was in doubt. Furthermore, as a coalition it was prey to internal disputes, and constant tension between the Liberal Prime Minister and his Conservative colleagues over domestic, foreign, and imperial affairs. Lloyd George himself, a remote, Olympian figure, preoccupied with international peace conferences, aloof from the House of Commons, a Prime Minister without a party, an adventurer careless in his financial and sexual activities, was not one who inspired universal trust or affection. So the consensus of the armistice period soon evaporated and new conflicts took its place.

A series of challenges was launched which gradually undermined the coalition's claim to govern. New patterns were being formed which would shape the course of British history for the next twenty years. On the left, Lloyd George was bitterly attacked by many Liberals over his casualness towards old and hallowed principles such as free trade. His policy in Ireland appeared even more shocking since the British government pursued war against the IRA in 1919–21 with an unrestrained policy of retaliation which led to bloody atrocities being committed by the auxiliary forces that were maintained by the Crown to back up the army and the constabulary. In December 1921, Lloyd George, always by instinct a negotiator, eventually made peace with the Sinn Fein leaders, Arthur Griffith and Michael Collins. From January 1922, an Irish Free State, consisting of the twenty-six Catholic counties of southern Ireland, was created, with just the six Protestant counties of Ulster in the north-east left within the United Kingdom. But this volte-face was too late to repair Lloyd George's tarnished image amongst liberal opinion. In the Labour Party and trade union world, the Prime Minister totally lost the reputation he had long enjoyed as a patron of labour. His government used tough methods, including emergency powers and the use of troops as strike-breakers, in dealing with national strikes by miners, railwaymen, and many other workers (including even the police) in 1919–21. Thereafter, the government failed to prevent massive unemployment (soon rising to over a million workers) from growing up and casting a blight over the older industrial areas. Episodes like the apparent deceiving of the coal-miners over the Sankey report and the proposed nationalization of the mines in 1919, and the further undermining of the 'Triple Alliance' to frustrate the miners again on 'Black Friday' (15 April 1921) sank deep into the consciousness of the working class. A government elected to promote national solidarity and social unity had made the class divide wider than ever before. If the coalition was attacked on the left, it was increasingly under fire on the right as well. Conservatives longed for the return of a healthy system of independent party politics, freed from the buccaneering methods of an autocratic Prime Minister and his retainers. Although the coalition hung on for almost four years, it was in dire straits and Lloyd George himself a Prime Minister at bay.

Above and beyond all this, there was a wider mood of disillusion with the peace treaties and the 'system of Versailles'. The peace settlement was increasingly unpopular. It was linked with covert secret treaties concluded during the war between Britain and its allies, and with unjust terms, for financial reparation and frontier arrangements, imposed on the defeated Germans. No book more effectively expressed this mood than did the economist J. M. Keynes's *Economic Consequences of the Peace* (1919). The work of a financial adviser to the Treasury who had resigned in protest during the Paris peace conference, it rapidly became a best seller on both sides of the Atlantic. It seemed to show conclusively that the reparations imposed on Germany would lead to its financial ruin and thereby to the permanent weakening of European economy. Keynes also evoked, in memorable and picturesque language, the frenzied, corrrupt atmosphere in which the various covert bargains were struck by the peacemakers in Versailles. Lloyd George was condemned as a man 'rooted in nothing'. The premier's efforts to act as the peacemaker of Europe in successive international conferences became unpopular. Britain refused any longer to act, in Bonar Law's striking phrase, as 'the policeman of the world'. The empire might be larger than ever, but it must be accompanied by a withdrawal from commitments in Europe. Otherwise another tragedy would afflict the land as it had done in August 1914. The final blow for Lloyd George's coalition came in October 1922 when it seemed that Britain was on the verge of war with Turkey over the defence of the Greek position in Asia Minor and protection of the Straits. Conservatives as well as the British left revolted against this rekindling of jingoism. The right-wing basis of the government collapsed. Lloyd George fell from power on 19 October 1922, a political pariah for the rest of his life.

Two kinds of reaction against Lloyd George's government followed. They were symbolized respectively by Ramsay MacDonald and Stanley Baldwin, both prominent in the movements that led to the downfall of the coalition in October 1922. MacDonald, with his heady Utopian internationalism and 'Brave New World' idealism, was the perfect voice for the growing Labour Party, whose tally of seats rose rapidly in the 1922 and 1923 general elections. He could straddle both the socialism of Clydeside and the social conventions of the London establishment. Alternatively, and more influential still, Stanley Baldwin led the Conservative forces of suburban middle-class respectability and of orthodox patriotism, all alarmed at Lloyd George's political experiments and the international adventurism of British foreign policy after the war. Baldwin, Prime Minister in 1923–4, 1924–9, and 1935–7, was an appropriate leader for a Britain desperate for a return to tranquillity and social peace.

There was constant flux and upheaval in other spheres of public life as well. Many of the settled patterns of pre-war now seemed under assault. In Wales and Scotland there were small movements of intellectuals, which suggested that the very unity of the kingdom could itself be threatened. Two small nationalist parties were formed on the Irish model, Plaid Cymru in Wales in 1925 and the National Party of Scotland in 1928. However, their significance was to lie in a distant future. In the arts, in literature, music, painting, and architecture, the surviving presence of pre-war giants such as Kipling and Hardy, Elgar and Lutyens masked the underlying challenge of avant-garde movements expressive of 'modernism' and revolt. Amongst the novelists, the main work of Joyce and of D. H. Lawrence had already been written; indeed after *Women in Love* appeared in 1920, with its echoes of the *malaise* of the war years, Lawrence's later work seemed relatively unimpressive.

More innovative were the writings of the coterie of intellectuals and artists linked with the 'Bloomsbury group'. In
particular, the remarkable series of 'stream of consciousness'
novels produced by Virginia Woolf, with their subtle delinea-
tion of human character and strangely fluid form, testified to
the vitality of 'modernism' in the novel. More orthodox was
E. M. Forster's *Passage to India* (1924), the work of a novelist
indirectly associated with Bloomsbury, which, in its treatment
of the interaction of Western and Eastern cultures, portrays the
declining self-confidence of Western liberal humanism. The
most notable pioneering development in poetry was T. S. Eliot's
'The Waste Land' (1922) with its disturbing rhythms and im-
agery; its pervading tone of Christian resignation and private
melancholy captures one powerful aspect of the culture of the
twenties. It was not a creative time for the theatre other than
Shaw's *St. Joan*, his most powerful philosophic affirmation.
Nor was it an age of great imagination in art, design, and
architecture either; painters like Ben Nicholson were still seeking a new style, while others such as Paul Nash were apparently
marking time. In the world of art, the Bloomsbury group again
provided a few notable rebels, Roger Fry, the art critic and
patron, painters such as Duncan Grant and Vanessa Bell, trying
to break out of the mould of realism in pictorial representation.
Bloomsbury, indeed, with its writers and artists, and associated
figures like the economist J. M. Keynes, the essayist Lytton
Strachey, and its philosopher-mentor G. E. Moore, embodied
many of the strengths and limitations of the British cultural
scene in the twenties. It genuinely attempted to infuse British
art with the inspiration of the modernist poets and surrealist
artists of continental Europe. It combined the cult of the new
with an effective iconoclasm, most popularly conveyed in Lytton Strachey's satirical studies of the feet of clay of leading
Victorian personalities, from the queen downwards. More
negatively, Bloomsbury encouraged an inbred, almost tribal,
view of artistic communication; it became in time a sheltered
enclave with dynastic overtones. Writers in the thirties were to

criticize the Bloomsbury group as a new cultural establishment. They attacked them for laying insufficient emphasis on moral (rather than purely aesthetic) sensibility and for their supposed lack of political or public concern. Probably the Bloomsbury ethos encouraged a tendency for the art of the classes and masses to grow further and further apart.

Developments in the arts, however, with their expressions of revolt and emancipation, chimed in with wider social movements of the time. The women who gained the vote, partially in 1918 and then (conclusively) in 1928, were able to enjoy other freedoms as well, the right to smoke, to enjoy new leisure interests such as the films, to pursue a more open and less constrained 'sex life', and to wear clothes that were spectacularly far less drab or puritanical. The 'bright young things' extolled in memoirs of the twenties, for whom the satires and plays of Noël Coward appeared to have been specifically written, were limited enough in their outlook. They were usually of middle- to upper-class background. They, or their friends, were strongly associated with the public schools, with Oxford and Cambridge. Oxford, in particular, became linked with a kind of free cultural self-expression, tending to decadence, nihilism, or both, just as it was to be identified (equally wrongly) in the thirties with anti-war protest. The older universities were probably far less influential in society at large than later myth-mongers alleged, but they merged into the experimental climate of a more formless, rootless world.

Certainly, the older arbiters of moral standards seemed to be suffering a crisis of authority after the war. Nowhere was this more apparent than amongst the churches, manifestly among the casualties of total war, with the possible exception of the Roman Catholics with their strongly Irish membership. The nonconformist chapels, moral beacons to many in the Victorian heyday, were now suffering from falling membership, declining funds, diminished authority. Even in their strongholds in Wales and the North, the chapels were in steady retreat. Not least, the challenges to Puritanism and Sabbatarianism that the war had produced severely undermined what sanctions the chapels could muster. The Church of England, too, maintained its established, national role with much difficulty after the war. Archbishops such as Randall Davidson and Cosmo Lang spoke in terms of the old cohesion and disciplines, but their message appeared increasingly ineffective. In a formal sense, Britain was still a recognizably Christian country. Its Church leaders were still honoured and respected, indissolubly bound to Crown and landed aristocracy. Sunday was still a day of tranquillity and gloom when the trains did not run, and shops and theatres were closed, as also were public houses in Wales and Scotland. The revision of the Anglican Prayer Book in 1927-8 produced furious public debate; the old battles between Anglo-Catholic and evangelical wings of the established Church were vigorously resumed. The identification of religion with middle-class values, with the family, the community, and a safe form of patriotism was still maintained. So, too, was the link of religion with the empire, notably through youth movements such as the Boy Scouts and the Church Brigade. The war itself encouraged a kind of secular religiosity, symbolized in the Cenotaph erected by Lutyens in Whitehall as a memorial to the war dead. And yet, for all the formal trappings to remind the people of their religious inheritance through the centuries, the impact and mystique of Christianity was clearly on the wane, especially among the post-war generation and ex-servicemen.

The inability of the churches significantly to influence the course of events was dramatically shown during the 1926 general strike. In that year, the terrible cycle of industrial decline, unemployment, and social bitterness led to the worst explosion of class conflict that Britain had yet known. The great strikes of 1919-21 had now passed away. The Prime Minister, Baldwin, called for 'Peace in our Time, O Lord'. But in the greatest industry in the land, coal-mining, tension remained high, with a background of wage cuts, dismissals, and falling living standards for mining families. In April 1926 the government refused to renew a subsidy to the mining industry. On 2 May Baldwin broke off negotiations with the TUC delegation. Almost by accident, the unions lurched into a general strike. For nine days (3–12 May) Britain was at a virtual standstill. Never before had the potential economic strength of the unions in challenging the government and the constitutional order been shown with more powerful effect. The Church leaders, with their call for conciliation, were impotent in the wings.

In practice, the general strike was peaceful enough. There was no violence directed against the many blacklegs (including many Oxford and Cambridge students who forsook their studies for the purpose) who drove buses and engaged in other strike-breaking activities. There was no violence either from, or directed against, the police or the armed forces. In the end the TUC suddenly called the strike off on 12 May, with industrial areas in Yorkshire, Cumbria, Tyneside, South Wales, and Scotland as solid as ever, and with several groups of key workers (such as power engineers) never called out at all. It was a complete defeat for the unions, and especially for the miners, who remained out on stike for several more bitter months. Britain's class war had been a brief, bloodless skirmish. For middle-class bystanders it had even been painless, and almost great fun.

Still, it is obvious that the divisiveness revealed and reinforced by the general strike was one powerful factor that survived to plague the unity of the nation over the next twenty years or more. In Britain's coalfields, memories of 1926, its triumphs and betrayals, were still a living reality as late as the national miners' strike of 1984–5. The general strike may have been shown to be ineffective in the circumstances of 1926, with the unions half-hearted and the government well prepared and (in the case of such ministers as Winston Churchill, the Chancellor) even belligerent. Nevertheless, 1926—'Year One' in the later recollection of one Welsh miner—did demonstrate the extraordinary loyalty and class solidarity within the working-class communities of Britain, not only in older mining, steel, and shipbuilding areas but also among the newer service workers of a 'semi-skilled' category in road or rail transport and distribution. The class divisions of the country were starkly revealed, even if they did not spill over into physical violence. A deep suspicion also was displayed about the alleged neutrality of the police or the civil service, even perhaps of the newly-formed BBC, which had in fact fought hard to preserve its independence in the face of governmental pressure. In mining districts, the general strike brought a legacy of victimization by mine-owners, swingeing wage cuts, and attempts to undermine the basic role of the Miners' Federation as voices of the workers. If demagogic miners' leaders such as Arthur Cook moved on to the sidelines, their successors in the unions and the Labour Party were no more accommodating towards a social system so manifestly distorted in its rewards and opportunities, and which made such a mockery of the supposed social unity of the war years. As Britain continued to limp through the depression years, memories of the general strike endured, and a heritage of class protest along with it.

In the later twenties, the land settled down into a pattern that endured until the 1940s. The population continued to grow, if more slowly; it rose from 40,831,000 in 1911 to 42,769,000 in 1921, and to 44,795,000 by the 1931 Census. But within it there were deep and growing contrasts, as younger writers such as George Orwell were later to emphasize. For much of southern England and the Midlands, the twenties were a time of growing contentment and prosperity. There were many housing developments in the form of suburban middle-class estates, stemming from the abortive Addison housing programme of 1919–21 and later schemes by Neville Chamberlain which gave a direct subsidy to private house-builders. A larger proportion of the population emerged from the war with middle-class aspirations—home ownership; a quiet family environment; more leisure pursuits (there were, for instance, over a million cars in private hands by 1930 of which the most celebrated was the 'Baby' Austin); domestic comforts and mechanical aids such as Hoovers. The power of broadcasting through the BBC brought entertainment and instruction into the privacy of the home. For the junior managers, civil servants, schoolteachers, skilled workers, and others, members of the white-collar administrative and professional groups that had expanded so dramatically between 1880 and 1918, the twenties were not such a bad time, with prices starting to fall, houses more freely available on easy terms, and more leisure interests to pursue. Newer technologically-advanced industries were mushrooming, notably the modern car plants of Herbert Austin at Longbridge and William Morris at Cowley, both in the Midlands. New patterns of suburban residential life flourished around them. For such people, the humdrum, reassuring values symbolized by the nature-loving Prime Minister, Stanley Baldwin, embodying in his own person the message of 'safety first', seemed attractive after all the unwanted excitements of the war and the general strike.

Yet for many other areas, it was a time of growing despair and disillusion. The countryside, for instance, was sunk in depression in the twenties after the brief, heady revival of the war years. The rural population steadily declined, especially in the more mechanized agricultural sector of the wheat-growing areas of southern England. Prices of farm products fell; the level of rural incomes declined; the vitality of small country towns, from the Highlands to Cornwall, became impoverished. British country life preserved its traditional unchanging appearance on the surface; the 'green revolution' vastly enlarged the number of small landowners in the 1918–26 period, the greatest transformation in landholding since the Norman Conquest. But beneath the surface was a pattern of indebtedness, burdens of mortgages and bank loans, and visible decay which saw the gap in the quality of life between town and country growing wider. Since much of British literature took the countryside as its basic point of reference, this could have serious cultural, as well as social, implications.

In the older industrial communities, especially in the north and north-east of England, industrial South Wales, and the

Clydeside belt of mid-Scotland, and in the slums of Belfast across the Irish Sea, it was a time of mounting despair. The inadequacy and squalor of working-class housing and living conditions became increasingly well documented in the twenties, as did the environmental decay that cast a pall over older areas such as Jarrow or Wigan or Merthyr Tydfil. Along with damp, insanitary housing and poor schools and public services went appalling figures of child illness and mortality, tuberculosis for the middle-aged, lung disease for miners, physical deformity for the old. There was a markedly lower life expectancy in the older industrial regions of the north, Wales, and Scotland, contrasted with the county towns and spas of the English south-east and the West Midlands. The social gulf grew ever wider in the twenties, made more severe still by the endless unemployment which afflicted older industries such as steelmaking, shipbuilding, and coal-mining, all of them starved of capital investment. The decision to return to the gold standard at the pre-war parity in 1925 was one taken by Churchill as Chancellor, in the face of biting criticism (after the event) from Keynes but with the broad endorsement of most orthodox economists and business men. It meant a serious overvaluing of British coal and steel exports, and a still higher rate of unemployment for the working men producing them. In terms of the quality of educational and medical facilities, of amenities such as libraries, swimming baths, or public parks, the social divisions were ever more apparent in the land over which Baldwin serenely presided. The era of 'safety first', with all its secularization, meant (according to some famous lectures by the socialist economic historian R. H. Tawney, published in 1929) the establishment of a new 'religion of inequality'. Among its features, two-thirds of the aggregate national wealth was owned by 400,000 people (less than one per cent of the population), along with immense disparities in the quality of life throughout British society.

Yet this growing social division occasioned surprisingly little revolt or protest at the time. In part, this was because of the warm solidarity of the working-class world which generated its own values, culture, and entertainment, even during the depression years. The relics of that period—the working-men's clubs and libraries; the vibrant world of the miners' lodge, the choir and brass band; the credit base provided by the 'co-op' in working-class communities—seem remote from the Britain of the 1980s. But they do testify to the strength and optimism of working-class life even in these gloomy years. The anodyne of mass entertainment was also encouraged by the rulers of the people to help promote patriotic loyalty. This 'bread and circuses' tradition dated from the Victorian music-hall. Many of its heroes such as George Robey (who had refused a knighthood) still flourished. But it was an art-form rapidly being outstripped by the new silent and talking pictures: Charlie Chaplin was now the darling of the halls. Beyond the innate resilience and dignity of working-class Britain, there were still qualities that kept the land relatively peaceful and integrated. These may have owed something to the much-maligned governments of the time. Neville Chamberlain's active and creative period as Minister of Health, 1924–9, which effectively saw the end of the old Poor Law, was one notable milestone in this process. The football crowds of the cloth-capped workers and the aspiring life-styles of the new middle class in the suburban housing developments were bound together by some semblance of common values. Familiar symbols could unite them all—perhaps the ever-popular figure of George V, perhaps the passive reassurance offered by Baldwin. The sporting hero of the decade was Jack Hobbs, opening batsman for Surrey and England, who in 1925 overtook the record number of centuries (125) scored by the legendary W. G. Grace. Modest, unprotesting, a devoted church-goer and teetotaller, a model family man, Jack Hobbs was the prototype of the loyal artisan dedicated to Crown and country. He was a professional 'player' content to be led by amateur public-school 'gentlemen' (who entered the Lord's playing arena by a different gate). He always played a straight bat and always accepted the umpire's verdict, however disappointing or unfair, without complaint. Jack Hobbs's placid, kindly personality provided an acceptable touchstone for a society struggling to preserve a traditional order in the swirling tides of the post-war transformation.

The Thirties

The twenties ended in a confused haze of nostalgia and innovation. The pomp and affluence of 'high society' and court life were as resplendent as ever. Cigarette cards and magazines acclaimed the personal appeal of social celebrities such as the aged tea magnate 'Tommy' Lipton or hostesses such as Lady Londonderry. Familiar giants still bestrode the land elsewhere. Elgar survived as Master of the King's Musick until 1934; Kipling remained actively writing until 1936; Thomas Hardy died, full of years and honour, in 1928. The mood of 'safety first' permitted only the most guarded forms of innovation. Its political figurehead in the later twenties was the Labour leader, Ramsay MacDonald, called upon to form a second Labour government in 1929. MacDonald had a background of anti-war protest in 1914–18, but as a reassuring figure in the general strike, the hammer of socialist extremists, and intimate of salons in high society, he seemed to be comfortingly locked within the aristocratic embrace. A licensed rebel, he was a safe enough symbol for a society committed to modest, but controlled, change. With Lloyd George now an isolated veteran and Churchill actively excluding himself from the Tory mainstream because of his 'die-hard' views on Indian self-government, MacDonald appeared to be a reliable guide in taking a few measured steps towards the apocalypse.

In fact, the second Labour government proved to be a disaster. In large part, this was because of forces far removed from political control. The crash in the American stock exchange in October 1929, followed by a downward spiral of trade and employment, was beyond the reach of any government to correct. For all that, it was all too apparent that the British Labour government had little to offer as a socialist or any other kind of palliative to unemployment that rose with alarming rapidity to reach nearly three million of the insured population at its peak in late 1932. Although unemployment gradually declined later in the thirties, in fact industrial stagnation and social decay continued. Beyond the world-wide forces of over-production and a slump in demand, there were factors peculiar to Britain alone. There was here an industrial structure unduly geared to a declining range of traditional industries, coal, steel, textiles, shipbuilding. There was a history of low investment, overmanning, and inefficient work practices, intensified by a culture that for decades had elevated humane disciplines and gentlemanly virtues in place of business education or entrepreneurial skills. The entire industrial and manufacturing base contracted with extreme violence. There was no sign of recovery visible until 1935. Long before then, the spectacle of hopelessness and despair in mining and other areas, of hunger marches and demonstrations by the unemployed, of the rigours of 'life on the dole' with all the helplessness and hopelessness that were implied had become one to which the great British public had become resigned or immune.

There were those who argued that a new kind of political initiative was required to regenerate and revitalize the nation and its economy, and to propel them in new directions. In the left centre, Lloyd George remained throughout the thirties an ageing, largely disregarded prophet, urging the need for a New Deal on the American model. On the far left, there were a variety of nostrums proposed, from the collectivism of the Socialist League, and later the Left Book Club, to the pure sectarianism of the tiny Communist Party. Sidney and Beatrice Webb claimed to see the future working in Soviet Russia. On the radical right, Sir Oswald Mosley left first the Conservative then the Labour Parties, and tried to create a British variant of Fascism with an admixture of corporate planning and anti-Semitism. Meanwhile the veteran socialist writers, Bernard

Shaw and H. G. Wells, in their different ways promoted the cause of a planned, antiseptic, scientific Utopia. But the most popular solutions were sought within the traditional mix of British politics. By August 1931 it was obvious that Mac-Donald's Labour government was in desperate straits. The climacteric arrived with a massive run on the pound accompanied by the publication of the May report which alleged that high government spending and an unbalanced budget were the root causes of industrial collapse. The government was urged to cut social spending, including the social benefit which was all that the unemployed had in order to subsist at all. The Cabinet was hopelessly divided, buffeted between the bankers and the TUC. On 23 August MacDonald resigned.

The next morning, however, instead of a Conservative–Liberal administration taking his place, it emerged that Mac-Donald was to stay on as Prime Minister of a new 'National' government from which almost all his own Labour Party colleagues would be excluded. At a subsequent general election in October, this government (which had latterly taken Britain off the gold standard and devalued the pound) was returned with a huge majority, with 556 supporters, and the Labour Party reduced to a mere 51, with almost all its leading former ministers defeated at the polls. This 'National Government' was to set the tone for Britain in the thirties. MacDonald, its figurehead, gradually faded from the scene, an increasingly pathetic personality. Baldwin lingered on until 1937. He was still able to summon up immense reserves of political and tactical skill, as when he pushed through a bill to grant more self-government to India in 1935, or in his total outmanœuvring of Edward VIII in 1936 when that uncrowned monarch flouted popular convention by seeking in vain to retain his crown and also to marry a divorced American woman, Mrs Simpson. But the main energy within the government came from a new technocratic style of Conservative, freed from the rural stereotypes of Victorian days. Dominant among them was Neville Chamberlain, heir to a famous Birmingham dynasty, the outstanding figure in political life in the thirties, at home and (later) abroad. Chamberlain it was who led a half-recovery of the economy in the earlier part of the decade, with much investment in housing and in consumer durables, and new affluence for advanced industrial zones of the East Midlands and southern England. Emigration from older regions such as South Wales, Durham, Cumberland, and Scotland was balanced by new growth in the suburbs and the centres of light industry. There was a distinctive managerial regulatory style in government, Britain's 'middle way' in economic policy. There were benefits for farmers in the form of milk and other marketing schemes and production quotas, and advantages for urban and suburban residents such as improved transportation (the London 'tube' being a notable example), extended gas and electricity services, and cheap housing. A century of free trade was buried at the Ottawa conference in 1932 when a new commercial system of tariffs and imperial preference, due to last until the 1970s, was inaugurated. The effect of tariffs upon the British economy was deeply controversial, but the cartelized steel industry was one industrial giant that appeared to show some benefit. The voters were duly grateful. They returned the National Government—now almost wholly Conservative—with a comfortable majority in the 1935 general election, and gave Chamberlainite managerial Conservatism a broad support until new divisions emerged over foreign policy at the end of the decade.

The politics of the National Government were based, unequivocally and unapologetically, on class and regional division. The older industrial areas were placed under the aegis of the 'special areas' schemes. In popular parlance, industrial Scotland, the north-east, Cumbria, much of Yorkshire and Lancashire, and South Wales were the 'depressed areas', self-contained societies only visible to the outside world when their refugees appeared in London and Birmingham to take part in hunger marches or to beg for coppers from theatre queues. There was an ironic, self-sustaining pattern about life in these so-called 'depressed' communities. There, industry was contracting, which meant that their rateable income fell further; this meant that amenities decayed still more, industrial decline was accelerated, and the entire, repetitive cycle became ever more severe. Some of the most powerful literature of the time— George Orwell's somewhat ambiguous saga of *The Road to Wigan Pier*, Walter Greenwood's pathetic account of *Love on the Dole*, Lewis Jones's moving treatment of life in Welsh mining villages in *Cwmardy* and *We Live*—evokes poignantly the consequences of this structural poverty upon the social and cultural sensibilities of the time. But little was done to remedy the causes. There were local philanthropic gestures by the Quakers and other idealists. There was some assistance from the government through the special areas commissions, although virtually nothing was done to diversify or overhaul the industrial base of these areas by a new regional policy. Thomas Jones ironically proposed that they might be turned into open-air archaeological museums, while trains carried off their inhabitants to the delights of employment at Dagenham or Hounslow. There were also novelties such as trading estates which offered inducements to industrialists to group together and move into older industrial areas by offering cheap rates or investment grants. The town of Slough in Buckinghamshire, for instance, became a focus for much industrial activity in the thirties—while its architectural horrors became the target for the unwontedly bitter satire of John Betjeman. But, in general, a combination of the constraints imposed by the Treasury and the Bank of England, and of a lack of urgency by government kept the areas of staple industry effectively without support. Not until the impact of rearmament in the period that followed the 1935 Defence White Paper, with its emphasis on engineering and aircraft production, was there a significant rise in employment.

But the main reason why so little stimulus was provided for the industrial regions crucified by depression was that they were self-contained and limited in extent. The majority of the population in other parts of Britain found that life after the holocaust was acceptable and in many ways agreeable. The thirties were a time of very low inflation, cheap private housing, and of a growing choice for consumers. An average of 345,000 houses was built annually between 1933 and 1937. The motor car industries, electrical, chemical, and textile concerns continued to thrive. In the Midlands, towns like Leicester and Coventry experienced unprecedented growth and affluence. The rewards of life were ever more apparent. Professional footballers for Herbert Chapman's Arsenal, though poorly paid, enjoyed a diet which included steak and champagne. In outer London, the spread of the 'tube', north towards Cockfosters on the edge of Hertfordshire, or west towards Uxbridge on the borders of Buckinghamshire, illustrated the expansion of the service and professional sectors of the white-collar population. In growing suburban communities such as Hendon, Harrow, or Kingsbury, there were smart shopping precincts, many new cinemas and football grounds. The untidy ribbon of semi-detached middle-class housing stretched far along arterial roads and bit deep into the surrounding countryside, relatively unhampered by environmental controls designed to preserve the 'green belts' around cities. The Western Avenue out of London became a byword for uncontrolled industrial and residential development, with a miscellany of factories in debased historicist styles (which a later generation, incongruously enough, often regarded as monuments of modern art). If one explanation for the lack of social change in Britain amidst the unemployment and depression of the thirties lies in the lack of political and economic power vested in the older industrial areas, another lies in the growing commitment to a pleasing and acceptable form of suburban life by larger and larger sections of the population left relatively unscathed by the bleak years.

Britain in the thirties, then, displayed a surprising degree of stability in a European continent which saw totalitarianism engulf Germany, Italy, and Austria, and the French and Spanish republics cast into disarray. The social and cultural hierarchy changed very little. The prestige of Parliament, of the law courts, of a highly stratified educational system headed by Oxford and Cambridge that remained almost totally a public-school preserve, all remained as high as ever. The monarchy retained its esteem by responding subtly to marginal changes in the outlook of the mass democracy: George V's attendance at the annual working-class festival of the Wembley Cup Final was one instance. The king's silver jubilee in 1935 provoked widespread national rejoicing. Even the brief crisis associated with the abdication of Edward VIII left the monarchy as an institution essentially unimpaired. The nation remained comfortably isolated from a strife-torn Continent, inhabited by far-away peoples of whom the British knew little.

In the arts, the thirties were in many ways a remarkably flourishing and creative period. In poetry, the most important figure remained T. S. Eliot, a conservative Anglo-Catholic of American birth, whose 'Four Quartets' appeared from 1930 onwards. Eliot, in fact, increasingly found the drama a more congenial art form, starting with *Murder in the Cathedral* (1935), a powerful commentary on the martyrdom of Thomas Becket. The most influential writers of the period, however, reacted strongly against what appeared to them to be the withdrawal and detachment of the Bloomsbury ethos in the twenties. In the maelstrom of the time, younger poets such as W. H. Auden, Stephen Spender, Cecil Day Lewis, and Louis MacNeice reflected the political excitements of the time. Auden's celebrated poem 'Spain' (1937), inspired by his brief period of service in the Civil War, epitomized the current literary mood. It is significant that all these young poets flirted with a kind of neo-Marxism, if they did not actually become Communists. Conversely, two of the abler young novelists of the time, Evelyn Waugh and Graham Greene, were converts to Roman Catholicism, albeit with very different political and other outlooks. British music was less volatile, though the romantic strains of Holst and Delius had to contend with the experimental en-

deavours, atonal, even unstructural, of the followers of Stra-
vinsky and Schoenberg. Vaughan Williams, a contemporary
enough figure in his diatonic compositional techniques, yet
deeply English in his reliance on traditional airs and themes,
demonstrated how modernity could be safely reconciled
with the native musical tradition. In the visual arts, the thirties
was a period of great excitement and innovation, both in sculpture and in painting. A new vitality for British sculpture was
heralded by the work of Henry Moore, son of a Yorkshire
miner, and the disciple of Epstein; another pioneer was Barbara
Hepworth, the wife of the painter Ben Nicholson. British painting was also unusually vigorous at this period, ranging from the
rustic Christian symbolism of Stanley Spencer to Paul Nash's
successful engagements with French surrealism. Britain was
generally a better country to look at in the thirties, with a
much-needed innovation in architecture and design, without
precedent since the heyday of Norman Shaw, Voysey, and
Mackintosh before 1914. From dramatic set-piece public buildings which manifested the influence of Gropius and the German
Bauhaus, through industrial factories and cinemas with *art
nouveau* or art deco overtones, down to mundane but important landmarks such as Pick and Holden's attractive new
underground railway stations for London Transport, British
architecture offered many departures and a real sense of liberation. At a more accessible level, the new life shown by the
Royal Academy and by such accepted popular arts festivals as
Sir Henry Wood's London 'proms' suggested some qualified
cultural advance, if hardly a cultural revolution.

In a variety of ways, then, Britain in the thirties showed
distinct signs, outside the older industrial areas, of being a land
at peace with itself, and enlivened by some cultural imagination. But the mood began to change abruptly in 1937, not
through any immediate domestic disunity or reappraisal, but
through the external impact of foreign affairs. Much of Britain's internal harmony in the twenties and thirties had been
founded on a quiescent foreign policy. The mood dictated by

Keynes in 1919, the mood that had dislodged Lloyd George in 1922, had permeated the whole society. Right-wing reluctance to engage in overseas military adventures was countered by a profound belief on the left that the 1919 peace settlement was in any case vindictive and morally indefensible, the product of national and imperial rivalries rather than of a yearning for a more harmonious world. In the twenties, Britain's defences were gradually run down, with little public protest, based on the 'ten year' premiss that no major war would be fought within the next decade. The battle fleet was especially cut back in this period, most enthusiastically by Churchill himself while at the Treasury. The giant new naval base at Singapore, recently completed, already seemed an anachronism. The main military commitment was to the Raj in India, but a gradual, partial accommodation with Gandhi and the Congress movement enabled the British garrison in the subcontinent to be reduced slowly from 57,000 in 1925 to 51,000 in 1938. Equally, the increasingly harmonious relations with the Irish Free State, culminating in the 'agreements' of 1936 and the virtual wiping out of all debts owed to Britain by Ireland minimized another potential source of military or naval difficulty. The public mood in the early thirties remained a passive one, even after the advent of Hitler in Germany in January 1933. The British labour movement was pacifist-inclined, with a few exceptions such as Ernest Bevin of the Transport Workers. It opposed voting arms estimates on behalf of a right-wing National government. On the socialist left, there were advocates of a Popular Front such as Sir Stafford Cripps who urged the need for an alliance with the Soviet Union and argued that socialism alone was the true remedy for international discord. Conversely, most Conservatives had no wish for an adventurous foreign policy, especially since Baldwin had assured the people that there was no real defence possible in a future war which would be determined largely by air power. The bomber would always get through. There was scant Conservative enthusiasm for upholding the authority of the League of Nations in crises in Manchuria in 1931 or Abyssinia in 1935. There were those on the right, notably some press lords, who declared that there was common ground between Great Britain and Hitler's Germany, bound together by Teutonic racial origins and anti-Communism. A miscellaneous group of politicians and journalists found a haven in Lord and Lady Astor's mansion at Cliveden, by the Thames, near Marlow. It was widely believed to be turning the mind of the Foreign Office in these fellow-travelling directions.

When the opportunity for action came, public opinion was resistant. Hitler marched into the Rhineland in early 1936, in direct contravention of the Versailles settlement. But only a few voices, like the isolated and unpopular Winston Churchill, called for a military response from Great Britain. Earlier, the British public had generally endorsed, though with much embarrassment, the appeasement policy of the Foreign Office following the Italian invasion of Abyssinia. In effect, the Italians were allowed to occupy this ancient empire in the Horn of Africa with the minimum of British involvement, economic or military. Formal commitments were made to the League and to the spirit of collective security, but they added up to little enough. Sir Samuel Hoare, the Foreign Secretary, was offered up as a public sacrifice during the Abyssinian crisis, but it was clear that the appeasement of Mussolini's Italy was a collective government decision. Cabinet records now available confirm the point. In any event, Hoare re-entered the government a few months later with little controversy. Again, in Spain where a left-wing, democratically-elected Republican government was subjected to invasion by a right-wing Nationalist force led by General Franco, with later armed assistance from Italy and Germany, the British government adhered rigidly to 'non-intervention', even if this meant the eventual downfall of democracy in Spain. The advent of the powerful figure of Neville Chamberlain in October 1937, a confident man committed to an active, positive pursuit of a working accommodation with the Fascist dictators, as opposed to Baldwin's passive style of appeasement, confirmed a growing mood of non-involvement in Europe. Key figures in the civil service such as Sir Horace Wilson and Sir Nevile Henderson (ambassador to Berlin) pushed this policy forward.

At various levels, however, the public mood suddenly began to change. Even the government began to turn its mind to the need to overhaul the national defences, especially in the air. From 1935 onwards, a new fighter-based air force was in the making, backed up by the latest technology invested in 'radar' and other anti-aircraft and defence systems. Through men like Tizard and his rival Lindemann, the voice of scientific innovation was again sporadically heard in the corridors of power. By 1937 the rearmament programme was visibly under way, despite pressure from the Treasury which voiced concern at the effect on the balance of payments. Privately, it is now known that a wider range of financial relationships was entered into with the United States which alone could underwrite the arms programme capable of being launched by a Britain still in economic difficulties. More widely, the public psychology was deeply stirred by events in the Spanish Civil War. Not only poets such as Auden or prose writers like George Orwell, but many scores of British working-class volunteers who fought with the International Brigade were being propelled towards a new commitment to internationalism. Jewish refugees from Germany brought the reality of Hitler's regime and of anti-Semitism home to British opinion. Even on the Labour left, trade union leaders such as Bevin and Citrine turned vigorously against neo-pacifist Labour politicians who denied armed assistance to trade union and labour groups crushed in Fascist Germany and Austria. Chamberlain's equilibrism was harder to sustain, especially for a Prime Minister so lacking in the skills of flexibility.

The German advance in 1938, the seizure of Austria and the subsequent threat to Czechoslovakia, ostensibly on behalf of the Sudeten Germans in the western fringe of Bohemia, produced a national crisis of conscience. Chamberlain responded with managerial decisiveness. At Berchtesgaden, Bad Godesberg, and finally at Munich in September 1938, he came to terms with Hitler. In effect, he allowed the Germans to annex Sudetenland on the basis of any timetable they chose, without British or French armed retaliation. For a brief moment, it seemed that this policy of surrender had mirrored the public's response. Chamberlain returned in triumph, announcing, in an ominous phrase, that it was to be peace in our time. But this abdication of responsibility could no longer adequately be justified. Those who have claimed that Chamberlain was seeking a breathing-space, in order for Britain to challenge Germany more effectively in military terms later on, do not find support from the records of Cabinet deliberations. The criticisms of Churchill and his associates, and even of Anthony Eden who had recently resigned from the Foreign Office in protest at Chamberlain's conduct of foreign affairs, now accorded far more precisely with popular sentiment. By the end of 1938, as it became clear that Munich had really meant the sacrifice of Czechoslovak democracy to armed aggression, nation-wide anger was overwhelming. Chamberlain, so impregnable a figure a few months earlier, the most powerful Prime Minister since Lloyd George in 1916, suddenly looked like a man on the run. Rearmament was stepped up and new negotiations begun with the engineering trade unions to try to build up munitions and aircraft production. When Hitler finally invaded Prague in March 1939, public anger exploded. Chamberlain was forced by outside pressure to enter into a military commitment to defend Poland, a land in Eastern Europe far away from British shores, with no guarantee that the Soviet Union would assist in protection of Poland's eastern frontiers. A century of almost unbroken British non-involvement in continental Europe, dating from the winding up of the Peninsular War in 1812, was abruptly reversed. The government was stampeded by a horrified public opinion. There was even a formal attempt to conclude an alliance with the Soviet Union, although things went so slowly that in the end Russia formed a pact with Germany instead in August. During the summer, there was evident a new mood of determination to resist German aggression with the full combined resources of the nation and the empire. On 1 September 1939 Hitler took the fateful step of invading Poland. After a few desperate attempts to patch up a last-minute compromise, Chamberlain announced in a broadcast on 3 September that Britain had declared war on Germany. There was scarcely any dissent, even from the tiny Communist Party, many of whose leading figures opposed the official Moscow line and took up the anti-Fascist cause. In the House of Commons, it was a Labour member, Arthur Greenwood, who 'spoke for England', and, as events showed, for virtually all of Wales, Scotland, Northern Ireland, and the dominions as well.

In the later stages of the appeasement controversy, the climate of public debate became unprecedentedly bitter. The complacency of the early thirties was set aside. There was the continuing hostility between the National government and the Labour Party over the unending tragedy of unemployment, and the scandals of the 'dole' and the operation of the 'means test'. Added to this was a powerful rift on the right between the 'men of Munich', Chamberlain, Simon, Hoare, and their followers, and the nationalist critics headed by Churchill who denounced the policy of craven appeasement as dishonourable. Episodes such as the distant impact of events in Czechoslovakia brought left- and right-wing protest together, as Spain or Abyssinia could never have done. Domestic and international conflicts merged into one passionate, turbulent whole. Chamberlain, the architect of much of the prosperity of the thirties, the titan of the suburban middle class, the dominant leader of the decade, suddenly became the hated symbol of a fraudulent, decadent political order. He became foremost among the 'guilty men' so brilliantly denounced by two young radical journalists, Michael Foot and Frank Owen, in a fierce polemic in 1940, perhaps the greatest feat of political pamphleteering since the days of Wilkes.

Any society ruled by Neville Chamberlain at such a time

should have found it hard to unite behind a common cause. Yet, as in August 1914, Britain did so. Indeed, when war broke out in 1939 there was a unanimity that pervaded all regions and classes. As in 1914, the war was represented publicly as a crusade on behalf of oppressed nationalities and persecuted races—which, indeed, it largely was, and far more plausibly so than in 1914. Middle and working class, capitalist and worker, socialist and conservative entered the war for different motives, or perhaps for different priorities along the political spectrum. But broad imperatives survived to create a new consensus. As twenty years earlier, Britain regained its sense of unity and national purpose amidst the challenge and turmoil of total war.

The Second World War

The public mood after the outbreak of the Second World War was notably less passionate or strident than after August 1914. Neither the militarism nor the pacifism of that earlier conflict was echoed now. In large measure, this was because of the curious features of the early months of the war. During the so-called 'phoney war' period down to April 1940, the fighting seemed remote, almost academic. It is a curious, twilight phase well portrayed in Evelyn Waugh's novel, *Put Out More Flags*. There were massive air-raid precautions, trenches in public parks, barrage balloons aloft, anti-aircraft weaponry deployed on public buildings. Thirty-eight million gas masks were distributed to men, women, and children; hundreds of thousands of schoolchildren were evacuated from major cities to distant, and presumably safer, rural areas (though many later drifted back home). Rationing of food, clothing, petrol, and other commodities suddenly became commonplace. The war itself was uneventful, with traditional pleasures such as the long-range enjoyment of a British naval victory, when the German battleship *Graf Spee* was fatally cornered by three smaller British vessels in the estuary of the River Plate off Montevideo harbour in late 1939. The uncertainty of the public mood was mirrored by the ambiguous nature of the government. Although the Cabinet had been reconstructed, to include Churchill himself, back at the Admiralty as in 1914, it was still the regime of the old gang, the National government of 1931 writ large. The trade unions in particular looked with deep suspicion at an administration still headed by their old adversary and class enemy, Chamberlain. Then in April 1940 the cold war hotted up. The Germans invaded Norway, scattering before them the British naval and military forces at Narvik. Soon afterwards, the Netherlands and Belgium were overrun, and the French army broke up in disorderly retreat. The security of the British Isles themselves was now under clear and pressing threat.

The old regime of the thirties could survive no longer. In a fateful division in the Commons on 7–8 May 1940, eighty Conservatives rebelled against the leadership of Chamberlain. Two days later he resigned, and Winston Churchill now emerged as wartime Prime Minister, with Labour and Liberals both joining the government. The change of premier was generally free of the apparent conspiratorial intrigue of December 1916. Indeed, Churchill had a vastly broader base of support in press and Parliament, and distinctly more loyalty from the military, naval, and air high command than Lloyd George had ever experienced. Churchill embodied a traditional sense of patriotic unity as no one else amongst his contemporaries could ever do. War gave his career a new impetus and relevance. His inspiring oratory over the radio and in the Commons conjured up new reserves of national will-power in this 'finest hour' for his country. He was able to exploit a humiliating military disaster in the retreat from Dunkirk as a kind of triumph for British ingenuity and determination. With France surrendering to the German forces by mid-June, British territorial security was threatened as never before since the days of Napoleon I in 1804.

The extent to which Britain was prepared to defend itself in military and naval terms is debatable. On the home front, apart from mobilized reserves, the 'home guard' of civilians was later to be effectively parodied as a 'dad's army' of amateurs muddling through with good humour. Its military effectiveness was, perhaps fortunately, never put to the test. But the real battle lay in the air, where the reserves of Spitfire and Hurricane fighter aircraft were rapidly built up by the press lord, Beaverbrook, now the Minister of Aircraft Production. From mid-August onwards, the German *Luftwaffe* launched wave after wave of blitz attacks, first on British airfields and aircraft factories, later on London, Coventry, Plymouth, Liverpool, Hull, Swansea, and other ports and major cities. Almost miraculously, civilian morale and national defences stood firm against this terrifying bombardment. In the air, the 'few', the legendary pilots of the Spitfires and Hurricanes, took heavy toll of the *Luftwaffe* in August–October. By Christmas, the threat of imminent invasion had effectively passed, though the 'blitz' on London and elsewhere continued. Churchill's personal reputation soared; the united spirit of his people grew with it. Dunkirk and the Battle of Britain in the air launched a thousand myths. They helped to encourage a latent isolationism and an unjustified feeling of national self-sufficiency, which led to a coolness towards Western European unity after the war. The British were aware that they alone of the belligerent Western democracies had escaped enemy occupation, as they had done consistently since 1066. For all that, the rhetoric of the 'finest hour' of 1940 captured the pride and the passion of what was felt to be a supreme moment of historic achievement.

The later course of the war on land, and more especially on sea and in the air, had a major long-term effect on the international and imperial status of Great Britain. It had begun by being a traditional European conflict to preserve national security and the balance of power in the West, to keep control of the Channel by extensive deployment of the British navy in the North Sea and in the northern Atlantic, along the western approaches. In effect, this aspect of the war reached a successful outcome by the summer of 1941, with the frustration of German threats to invade Britain (about which Hitler was always in any case hesitant) and the beating off of the *Luftwaffe* attacks. With the operations of the British merchant navy and (from early 1941) American lease-lend ensuring tolerable supplies of food and raw materials for the rest of the war, there was no imminent danger to the British Isles themselves, even though sinkings by German U-boats continued apace. Churchill kept a close eye on the ports of neutralist Eire and its anti-British premier, de Valera. The further hazards of guided missile attack by V1 and V2 machines, launched from bases in Holland in the summer and autumn of 1944, while deeply alarming and the source of much damage to life and property in south-east England, did not seriously imperil the security of nation either.

However, from late 1940, the war soon demonstrated wider, imperial themes. From being initially a conflict to preserve Western and Central Europe from the aggressive menace of German Fascism, the war rapidly turned into a broader effort to sustain the Commonwealth and empire as they had endured over the decades. The white dominions—Australia, New Zealand, Canada, and, far more hesitantly, South Africa—lent immediate support in terms of raw materials and armed naval and other assistance. In addition, the credits run up with India and Egypt in particular, the so-called 'sterling balances' which gave much trouble after the war, were vital in assisting with British payments for supplies, and in partially redressing the loss of overseas assets and the fall in 'invisible' income. The entry of the Soviet Union into the war in June 1941, and even more that of the United States in December 1941, following the Japanese assault on the US fleet at Pearl Harbor, ensured that the war would remain a worldwide one, fought in every continent and every ocean, and that the cosmic structure of the British Empire would come under acute threat.

Much British military, naval, and air-force effort was put into preserving the traditional lines of communication in the Middle East, centred on the Suez Canal, and the bases of the Persian Gulf and its hinterland, with their huge oil reserves.

British forces fought with much success to put pressure on the Italians in Abyssinia and Somaliland, after Italy entered the war in August 1940. Even more endeavour went into preserving Egypt and the north African littoral. In 1941 the British forces under Wavell captured the whole of Cyrenaica and advanced towards Tripoli, but were later forced to retreat back towards Egypt. The fall of Tobruk in early 1942 led to a major political crisis at home, in which Churchill's own position appeared under threat. The most important military engagement of later 1942 concerned the struggles of the British Eighth Army, under first Auchinleck then Montgomery, to resist a German advance towards Cairo and Suez. However, the final breakthrough by Montgomery at El Alamein in November 1942 resulted in a successful and sustained British drive across modern Libya, through Tripoli, and into Tunisia. Here, Montgomery linked up with the American armies under Bradley which had moved eastwards from the initial landing near Algiers. Subsequent allied campaigns, including the capture of Sicily and a prolonged drive through Italy, from the Anzio beach-head to the Alps, again had a strong concern with the imperial lines of strategic communication, and with control of the eastern Mediterranean. Those who argued that a second front should be launched in France in 1943, to relieve pressure on the Red Army in Russia, viewed this concentration in the Mediterranean with much frustration and anger. However, Churchill's Mediterranean commitment prevailed. In 1944, British forces again landed in Greece both to drive out the Germans and to beat down a native left-wing movement, ELAS.

In the Far East also, the war involved desperate efforts to shore up the empire at its base. The invasion of the Japanese through China into Indo-China and the Dutch East Indies, including the capture of all the American bases in the Philippines, led Churchill to place the Far East, with the approaches to the Indian subcontinent, even higher than the Middle East in the military priorities. There were dreadful losses. The most fateful of all involved the sinking of the battleships *Prince of Wales* and *Repulse* by Japanese bombs and torpedoes on 10 December 1941. There followed a rapid Japanese advance through Malaya and on 15 February 1942 the surrender of over 80,000 British and empire troops in Singapore. This disaster, the result of grave miscalculations by the commanding officer, General Percival, and by Churchill himself (who under-estimated Japanese fighting power), was described by the Prime Minister in the House as 'the worst capitulation in British history'. It was a landmark in the fall of empire. Henceforth, for instance, Australia and New Zealand were to look to the USA for protection in the Pacific rather than to the imperial mother country. However, the disasters went no further. Japanese advances into Burma were held off, with such forces as Orde Wingate's 'Chindits' gaining immense acclaim. British rule in India, threatened by disaffection by the Congress movement within the subcontinent as well as by Japanese assault from Burma, was sustained. By late 1944, the British position in eastern Asia and the Pacific, even with the loss of Malaya, Singapore, and Hong Kong, was still a powerful one, even if dependent on American land and naval assistance.

At last in June 1944, with the final invasion of France from the Normandy beach-heads by Allied forces under the command of Eisenhower and Montgomery, the war again assumed a European aspect. British military tactics in this last phase have led to some controversy amongst military historians, especially the delays in pushing through northern France and the Low Countries. The airborne landing at Arnhem was a débâcle. Even so, in the end it was a rapid and triumphant campaign. It was General Montgomery who formally received the unconditional surrender of the German forces at Lüneburg Heath on 9 May 1945. Hitler himself had committed suicide a few days earlier. Japan also surrendered on 15 August after two atomic bombs had wrought huge devastation at Hiroshima and Nagasaki, killing over 110,000 people.

Throughout, the war etched deep into the national psy-chology, without raising either the doubts or the euphoric jingoism of the Great War of 1914–18. The most satisfying fact of all was that casualties were so much lighter in the six years of the Second World War than in the four years of slogging trench warfare in 1914–18. This time a total of 270,000 servicemen were lost in six years, as well as over 60,000 civilians killed on the home front in German air raids. The campaigns had been more peripheral, more episodic, and in the end far more effectively conducted on a technical basis. Even veterans of the peace movement such as the philosopher Bertrand Russell felt that here was almost a good war. At the same time, all the vital questions surrounding Britain's external role remained unanswered. In the Middle and Far East, supreme strains had been put on the imperial system, even if Britain assumed control again of territories such as Hong Kong, Sarawak, Malaya, and Singapore in Asia, and British Somaliland in Africa. The Americans were concerned, at war-time conferences and at the Potsdam peace conference of July–August 1945, to speed up the process of decolonization. Churchill was led to observe anxiously that he had not become the king's minister, or fought a bloody war for six years, in order to achieve the dissolution of the British Empire. But already his outlook was being overtaken by events.

On the home front, the impact of total war was scarcely less momentous. As in the earlier war, there was a vast upheaval in the pattern and structure of the population, and a new juggernaut of centralization and state control to regulate social and economic life. Unlike 1914–18, however, the apparatus this time seemed to operate with far more justice—and more likelihood of the momentum being continued into the post-war world. The war clearly expressed a profound spirit of egalitarianism, of a type previously unknown in British history at any period. George Orwell felt that a social revolution was taking place. The ration books, gas masks, identity cards, and other wartime controls afflicted the people equally and implied a mood of 'fair shares'. So did the communal sufferings during the blitz. A notable impact was achieved by the 'evacuees', the school-children removed from London, Birmingham, Liverpool, and other cities to take refuge in rural communities in England and Wales. For the first time, large sections of the nation got to know each other. The medical and food provision for the evacuated children of the urban slums meant a great improvement in their physical and mental well-being. For their parents, war miraculously meant that full employment was restored, after the terrible decay of the thirties. Egalitarianism also encouraged a new faith in social planning, even if the links between shop floor and pit-head and the drawing-board deliberations of London-based bureaucrats were not necessarily obvious or automatic. The result, however, was that, in the wartime mood of unity and equality of sacrifice, novel questions began to be asked about public policy. A profound conviction arose, equally amongst the armed forces, that this time the 'land fit for heroes' would not be so wantonly set aside as it was widely felt to have been in the years after 1918. This mood was captured with much precision by the wartime illustrated magazine, *Picture Post*, edited by Tom Hopkinson, by the newspaper the *Daily Mirror*, and by the popular radio talks of the Yorkshire author J. B. Priestley, whose Cobbett-like style of native radicalism achieved widespread appeal.

The most celebrated document of this mood was the Beveridge report of November 1942. The work of an austere academic economist, it outlined an exciting scheme of comprehensive social security, financed from central taxation, including maternity benefits and child allowances, universal health and unemployment insurance, old age pension and death benefits. It was, in the phrase of the time, provision 'from the cradle to the grave'. An ecstatic public response gave the uncharismatic Beveridge a new celebrity as another 'People's William'; it ensured that social policy would remain high on the public agenda after the war, along with other priorities such as a free national health service. The Barlow report (actually issued in 1940) visualized a complete overhaul of the stagnant 'depressed areas'. Subsequently the 1945 Distribution of

Industry Act began a long-overdue process of reversing the economic decline of areas such as north-east England and South Wales by diversifying and modernizing their economic infrastructure. The Uthwatt report of 1942 outlined a new dynamic approach to town planning with 'green belt' provision around major conurbations, new controls over land use, and 'new towns' to cater for the overspill of older cities. Underlying all these wartime blueprints was a commitment to full employment, spelt out in the 1943 budget and a government White Paper of 1944. The tragedy of stagnation and economic and human waste that had crucified many communities in the thirties would not be repeated. Spokesmen for the unemployed marchers then, people like 'Red Ellen' Wilkinson, MP for Jarrow and leader of the 1936 Hunger March, were now active in government. Underpinning this vogue for social innovation was the transformation of fiscal policy, with a commitment to counter-cyclical policies, a manpower budget, and the management of demand. These were taken up even by such traditionalist wartime Chancellors as Kingsley Wood and Sir John Anderson. Keynes himself served at the Treasury and greatly influenced the powerful Economic Section of the Cabinet. The leading critic of the post-war settlement of 1919, he was now a key figure, not only in domestic budgetary policies, but also in external financial arrangements including the attempt to rationalize international trade and currency through the Bretton Woods agreement. The most radical nostrums were now proposed in the most staid of circles: nationalization of major industries and the Bank of England; a levy on inherited capital; a salaried state-directed medical profession. They all provoked growing arguments between Conservative and Labour Cabinet ministers, with angry sniping from the back-benches by freebooters such as Emanuel Shinwell, a forthright Glasgow Jew, and Aneurin Bevan, a brilliant Welsh ex-miner. But such a flowering of social and intellectual debate, far more precisely conceived and of far wider appeal than the 'reconstruction' discussions of 1917–18, under the aegis of such a traditional wartime leader as Churchill, was indeed a sign of a new climate.

In culture and the arts, the war gave some new life to old values. Literature, significantly enough, was not stimulated to anything like the same degree as in 1914–18; there was nothing remotely resembling the generation of 'war poets' of that earlier period. Some encouragement was given to war artists, officially sponsored to depict experiences in the blitz and elsewhere: Henry Moore, John Piper, and Graham Sutherland are three notable examples. Interestingly, music was one art form given a powerful stimulus, especially through the patronage of the wartime creation of CEMA (Council for the Encouragement of Music and the Arts). Lunchtime piano concerts in London during the blitz by Dame Myra Hess suggested a new popular enthusiasm for music. The composers' response came in powerful creations by Michael Tippett (a pacifist who produced a moving and humane work, *A Child of Our Time*) and the work of Benjamin Britten. The latter's *Peter Grimes*, first performed in June 1945, gave a remarkable new vitality to English opera, still largely derived from the light concoctions of Gilbert and Sullivan fifty years earlier. During the war also, the cinema became more recognizable as an innovative art form. Films such as *In Which we Serve* and *Brief Encounter* drew effectively upon wartime themes—separation, loss, sacrifice—to imbue a commercially-inclined industry with some creative realism. Of all the media for cultural communication, however, it was BBC radio which loomed largest in the public mind. Comedians like Tommy Handley, popular singers like Vera Lynn, war reporters like Richard Dimbleby and Wynford Vaughan Thomas, became the great mass entertainers and communicators of their time. In a world convulsed by unfamiliar social and intellectual ideas, the BBC remained a basically conservative, reassuring institution, committed to God, the king, and the family, to the continuities of life and the permanence of the national heritage. In the holocaust of six years of war, that appeared to be what the mass populace required and demanded.

It was, in any case, an increasingly aware and educated populace. British education had not undergone any major overhaul since 1918; its expansion had been cruelly cut back by the Geddes economies of 1922. Large sections of the working-class community had virtually no secondary schooling at all, while the proportion attending university or other higher education down to 1939 was extraordinarily small by international standards, and almost entirely of wealthy or middle-class background, save only in Wales. Hence the Butler Education Act of 1944, another social landmark of the war years, laid the framework of a new comprehensive secondary system for all, divided like Gaul into three parts, secondary modern, grammar, and technical. At the same time by giving new life to the grammar schools, and outlining a vast future investment in school building and equipment, it helped ensure a far greater degree of literacy and of social and occupational mobility. In the post-war world, the age of the grammar-bred boy and girl would surely dawn, whatever doubts surrounded the standards of the 'modern' schools which the unsuccessful majority would attend.

The First World War had produced an official commitment to the restitution of traditional values and ideas, whatever the mass popular enthusiasm for social change, or even revolution, both in working-class circles and intellectual coteries. The Second World War saw far less division between aspiration and reality. Indeed, the congruence between a public commitment to change and a private administrative recognition that pre-war society was dangerously unjust and divisive was the most important legacy of the Second World War for the British people. One major aspect of this was that the trade unions were now very far from being the outsiders that they had been after 1918. The most powerful union leader of the day, Ernest Bevin of the Transport and General Workers, was the dominant government minister on the home front, after Churchill appointed him Minister of Labour in May 1940. Under his aegis, the unions worked with government in regulating working practices, in improving industrial conditions, and in the strategy of economic planning with an intimacy never before achieved. Walter Citrine, secretary of the TUC, became virtually an ancillary member of the government. There were indeed strikes during the war, notably among miners in Kent in 1942 and among boy apprentices on the Clyde in 1941 and in South Wales in 1942–3. But they were relatively minor events contrasted with the wider consensus that was emerging. By the end of the war in 1945, the TUC had drafted a revised list of public priorities, including the nationalization of major industries and public services, the maintenance of full employment, a welfare state on the lines of the Beveridge report, and a more egalitarian financial policy based on the wartime ethos of 'fair shares'.

At all levels this feeling chimed in with a noticeable mood of political radicalism. Indeed, in the years 1940–5, Britain may be said to have moved more rapidly to the left than at any other period of its history. In government, Labour ministers of the Churchill administration loomed large on the home front. Ernest Bevin; Clement Attlee, the deputy Prime Minister; Herbert Morrison, the Home Secretary; Greenwood, Dalton, and others became familiar and trusted figures. They were talismans of the faith that post-war reconstruction would indeed be carried into effect. So, too, were reformist Conservative ministers such as R. A. Butler, author of the Education Act. Their outlook harmonized with the new orthodoxies of the planners, many of them Liberal theoreticians such as Keynes or Beveridge, or simply apolitical technocrats. Beyond the confines of Westminster and Whitehall, it was clear that the public was becoming more radical—at least, it should have been clear, since this was documented in Gallup polls in the newspapers, though little attention was paid by contemporaries to these unfamiliar forms of sociological evidence, of transatlantic origin. In by-elections, there were several successes for the vaguely Christian socialist Common Wealth Party. There was the widespread public enthusiasm for the Red Army, newly popular after Stalingrad and the advance towards Berlin. Even in the armed forces, so it was murmured, left-wing or novel ideas were being bandied about in current affairs groups and discussion circles. Letters home from servicemen in the western desert or the Far East voiced the angry determination for a better deal in the post-war world.

Reconstruction, then, was a far more coherent and deep-rooted concept as the war came to its close. In 1918, many of the blueprints had been poorly-conceived and destined for rapid oblivion at the hands of the Treasury. This time it had been more plausibly a people's war. The ideas were more precise and had both more democratic impetus and more intellectual ballast behind them. The outcome was revealed with dramatic effect as soon as the war ended. The Churchill coalition broke up with unexpected suddenness in May 1945, a few days after the German surrender and with hostilities still continuing in the Far East against the Japanese. To Churchill's dismay, the Labour Party's national executive, voicing the wishes of the rank and file, insisted that Labour's ministers leave the government. A general election was called for July. The 'coupon election' of 1918 had been an unreal exercise throughout. Even if not polluted by the hysterical 'hang-the-Kaiser' jingoism to the extent that Keynes had suggested, that element was undoubtedly present. A general patriotic exaltation made the campaign of November–December 1918 a poor guide to the public mood. In June–July 1945, however, the spirit was more sober and focused more precisely on housing and health, full employment, and industrial regeneration, on post-war social imperatives rather than on external or imperial themes. In this sense, the power and prestige of Winston Churchill, the revered war leader, were an irrelevance, even an embarrassment to the Conservative Party. The result, to the general astonishment, was a political landslide without precedent since 1906. Labour made 203 gains and won, in all, 394 seats to the Conservatives' 210. Clement Attlee, the prosaic, reticent leader of the Labour Party, found himself propelled into 10 Downing Street, at the head of a government elected with a massive majority. Alongside were such experienced figures as Ernest Bevin as Foreign Secretary, Herbert Morrison as deputy Prime Minister, Hugh Dalton at the Treasury, and Sir Stafford Cripps at the Board of Trade. It was a striking comment on the changed atmosphere of the war years, and no doubt a delayed verdict on the bitterness of the thirties, with its memories of Munich and Spain, Jarrow and the hunger marches. For a rare moment in its history, Britain appeared to present a spectacle of discontinuity and disjunction. It left ministers and the mass electorate at the same time exhilarated and bewildered. As James Griffiths, one new Labour minister, exclaimed in genuine bewilderment at the deluge, 'After this—what?'

The Post-War World

In fact, one phase of continuity was to be followed by another. The Labour government of 1945–51, while productive of much domestic partisanship and occasional bitterness during its six years of office, launched a new kind of consensus, a social democracy based on a mixed economy and a welfare state which took Britain well enough through the difficult post-war transformations and endured in its essence for another generation or more. Not until the very different political and economic climate of the later 1970s did the Attlee-based consensus which emerged from the post-war period come to be challenged. Until then, the balance between innovation and stability that the post-1945 regime introduced seemed to conform to the general will.

At one level, the Attlee government certainly brought about a remarkable programme of sustained reformist activity. Major industries and institutions were brought into public ownership—coal, railways, road transport, civil aviation, gas, electricity, cable and wireless, even the Bank of England. In all, 20 per cent of the nation's industry was taken into the 'public sector'. Remote groups of corporate private capitalists were replaced by remote boards of corporate public bureaucrats. Not until the nationalization of iron and steel in 1948–9 brought differences within the government to the surface did the main premises of public ownership, as spelt out in the 1945 Labour manifesto, come to be challenged. There was also the great extension of publicly-financed social welfare, popularly dubbed 'the welfare state'. The most spectacular and controversial feature of this was the National Health Service introduced by Aneurin Bevan in 1946, and coming into effect in July 1948. The Health Service generated much debate at the time, and much resistance by the doctors who viewed with alarm attempts to implement a salaried system to make them state employees, and to abolish the sale of private practices. However, the public consensus after the war was sufficiently powerful to force the bill through, and to enable free medical attention for all citizens to come into effect. Other notable measures included the national insurance system introduced in 1946, very much on the lines of Beveridge's wartime proposals; a new drive for state-subsidized 'council' houses which yielded well over a million new and temporary dwellings up to 1952; increased old age pensions; a raising of the school-leaving age; and child allowances. These measures were by no means greeted with such unanimous acclaim at the time as is sometimes alleged. The government made many concessions to its critics. Bevan himself had to allow the retention of private practice by the medical profession, and 'pay beds' within the nationalized hospitals, a typically British compromise. In secondary education, the public schools flourished side by side with the state grammar schools. Indeed, the years of socialist rule after 1945 saw Eton and other privately-endowed educational institutions never more thriving, with their charitable status protected by the Inland Revenue. Public housing schemes were whittled down by pressures to encourage homes for sale and the principle of a 'property-owning democracy'. With all its limitations, however, the welfare state gained a broad measure of support, and was accepted as a vital attribute of the balanced, compassionate society over the next twenty years. Despite a ministerial fracas in April 1951, which led to the resignation of Aneurin Bevan and two other ministers over charges on dentures and spectacles, the underlying principles of a publicly-supported, comprehensive welfare state survived largely unscathed. So, too, did the commitment to full employment and new regional policies that gave renewed life to once derelict areas such as the Welsh valleys, Durham, Cumberland, and the central industrial belt of Scotland. In the light of these benefits, trade unionists were prepared to accept wage freezes, devaluation, and disagreeable hardships. Their loyalty to their own government survived all rebuffs.

Later legend made this era one of austerity and general gloom. So in some ways it was. From the outset, Britain faced a huge post-war debt. There were continuous shortages of raw materials and of basic food supplies, made worse by the lack of dollars which led to a severe imbalance of trade with North America. There were moments of near-panic like the run on sterling, following convertibility of the exchanges, in July 1947; the decision to impose devaluation of the pound against the dollar in September 1949; the balance of payments difficulties during the Korean War in July–August 1951. Rationing for food, clothing, petrol, and many domestic commodities survived until 1954. Planning and controls, administered by faceless bureaucrats in Whitehall (and circumvented by 'spivs' and the 'black market'), became part of the conventional stereotypes of the time. For all that, most working-class people, the vast majority of the population, viewed the years since 1945 as much the best that had been generally known since the late-Victorian heyday. Wages rose to 30 per cent above their 1938 level. There were higher living standards, guaranteed employment, more satisfying environmental and educational facilities. In a world, too, where popular sport such as football and cricket, and also the cinema and the dance-hall, were readily accessible, the leisure aspects of the good life were catered for as well. Football stadiums such as Highbury, Villa Park, or Old

Trafford attracted each week over 60,000 enthusiastic (and entirely peaceable) spectators. In 1951, in its last few months in office, the Labour government launched a Festival of Britain, to commemorate the centenary of the Great Exhibition of 1851. At a time of economic shortages and much gloom in overseas affairs, it seemed to some jaundiced critics hardly the right time for a festival of national rejoicing. But the Festival proved a triumphant occasion. It led, amongst other benefits, to a dramatic cleaning-up of the derelict south bank of the Thames, focusing on a superb new Festival Hall for music and other arts. It released new powers of creativity for architects, sculptors, and designers. At the same time, it suggested also some of the technological and manufacturing skills latent in the British people. Along the Thames at Battersea, the fun fair was a riot of gaiety and invention. The Festival was testimony to a people still vital and vigorous in its culture, still at peace with itself and secure in its heritage.

In fact, the buoyancy implied by the Festival of Britain was more than sustained by the Conservatives after 1951. Churchill, Eden, Macmillan, and Douglas-Home, the Prime Ministers during the period of unbroken Tory rule from 1951 to 1964, pursued a policy of social peace. The trade unions were generally permitted to develop their freedoms and collective bargaining powers that they had strengthened during the war. There were few major strikes, and no domestic violence, even in Northern Ireland. The welfare state was reinforced, with relatively few incursions into its provisions. Full employment remained a broad priority; indeed, it was thought to be ensured in perpetuity by the Keynesian methods of demand management symbolized in the financial creed of 'Mr Butskell' (a hybrid of the Tory Butler and the Labour leader, Gaitskell, which suggested the centrist policies of the time). When unemployment again reared its head in 1959–60, the Conservatives were as vigorous in promoting interventionist regional policies as their Labour predecessors had been. The Prime Minister of this period, Harold Macmillan, was dubbed

'Supermac' by the (half-admiring) left-wing newspaper cartoon-ist, 'Vicky'. There was, therefore, no major departure from Attlee-style consensus between 1951 and 1964. The return of another Labour government under Harold Wilson by a narrow majority in 1964—confirmed by a much larger majority in 1966—suggested no great deviation from the broadly-accepted political and social framework of the past twenty years.

Political harmony at home gave scope to experiment and innovation in the arts. After a barren decade in the 1940s, the fifties saw major works from many novelists of distinction, several of whom had begun writing before the war: Joyce Cary, Lawrence Durrell, Angus Wilson, and Iris Murdoch were among the most significant. British drama also experienced a renaissance at this period, from the avant-garde work of the Irishman Samuel Beckett, and of Harold Pinter, to the social realism of committed figures such as John Osborne. The latter's *Look Back in Anger* (1956), performed at the radical strong-hold of the Royal Court theatre in Sloane Square, created a stir with its contemptuous rejection of social change in Britain since 1945. The ambiguous, romantic phenomenon of the 'angry young man' was born. In *The Outsider*, Colin Wilson captured the dilemma of the alienated intellectual. Poetry also showed much vitality, notably through the Welsh poet Dylan Thomas, until he drank himself to death in New York in 1953 while on a trip to the United States. There was also the 'Ulster Renais-sance' in Northern Ireland. Beyond the shores of Britain, British visitors to the United States noted the near-monopoly of British dramatists and actors on Broadway. The illusion was nourished that Britain, for all its acknowledged economic weakness and technical backwardness, could still, through its cultural attain-ments, play Greece to America's Rome.

British music was also unusually lively, with Britten in par-ticular active both in composition and in opera, and older figures like Walton also vigorous. What was perhaps more encouraging was that music-making showed clear signs of being a less esoteric or middle-class activity. School orchestras and amateur music groups flourished. Local festivals were springing up apace, with the one launched at Edinburgh in 1947 the most distinguished. A major factor in all this was state patronage through the Arts Council, however much controversy its presence and influence aroused. One area where there was less evidence of advance, unfortunately, was architecture and town planning. The 'new towns' were mostly bywords for grim, Stalinist uniformity, while opportunities to rebuild older cities ravaged in the blitz were too often cast aside, notably in Manchester and the City of London around St. Paul's. Ugly, high-rise flats pierced the skyline. New civic buildings and universities were often severe and unattractive. 'Plate glass' was not a concept that commanded enthusiasm, and the design of major urban centres and older cathedral cities suffered accordingly.

Elsewhere in the arts world, the BBC, in both radio and, to a much lesser degree, television, showed signs of being cultural pioneers. The Third Programme became from 1946 a powerful stimulus to music and drama. Television became a nation-wide phenomenon after 1950, and, with all its admitted limitations, served a useful social role in introducing the nation to itself. The BBC was also valuable in catering for the interests of minorities, including intellectuals, speakers of Welsh, and Asian and other coloured immigrants. The cinema also gradually became a medium for renewed artistic experimentation. It was fortified by the mass audiences that its low prices and informal atmosphere were able to attract, and its immediate freedom from the rival challenge of television. The most notable film events of the late 1940s were the Ealing Studios' comedies, distinctive for their reinterpretation of traditional British themes with restrained humour and gentle tolerance. *Passport to Pimlico*, *Kind Hearts and Coronets* and others of this genre were testimony to the continuities and coherence of British society. Far less interesting were endless films produced in the shadow of the British class system, which depicted the working class in the affectionate, patronizing, uncomprehending terms familiar to West-End theatre-goers over the generations.

Foreigners were usually suspect or simply comic (as they were in the children's books of Enid Blyton which poured forth at this time). Enduring symbols such as the friendly village 'bobby' were given sentimental currency in the film *The Blue Lamp* or in television serials. More positively, in the later fifties, some of the new tides sweeping through the French, Italian, and (to some degree) the American cinema had some real impact on Britain also. A wave of socially realistic films, often with sharp social comment to offer, suggested a shift in cultural attitudes. The popularity of *A Taste of Honey* or *Saturday Night and Sunday Morning*, with their searching penetration of working-class values and the human relationships moulded by them, implied a new depth and sensitivity in the British cinema industry. At a wider level, it suggested the security and stability of Britain at this transitional period in its history.

The stability of the domestic scene was much assisted by the general quietude of external policy. Britain in 1945 was still a great power, one of the 'Big Three' at the international peace conferences. It demonstrated the fact by manufacturing its own atomic and hydrogen bombs. Until the cumulative effect of economic decline took its inevitable toll, this façade was preserved up to the Moscow Test-Ban Treaty of 1963. Britain had its own powerful defence systems, its own supposedly independent nuclear weaponry, its own sterling area, its private strategic, trading, and financial ties with a mighty, if dissolving, empire. In medical, physical, and chemical science, Britain was still pre-eminent, as the international acclaim for such Nobel prize-winning pioneers as Fleming and Florey, Crick and Watson suggested.

However, Britain's international position was qualified by the gradual, but necessary, retreat from empire that the post-war period witnessed. It was a relentless process, even during the regime of such a veteran imperialist as Sir Winston Churchill. The granting of self-government to India, Pakistan, Burma, and Ceylon (Sri Lanka) by the Attlee government in 1947–9 was the key moment in the transfer of power. It was an

FRANCE ITALY
PORTUGAL SPAIN
Gibraltar
Mediterranean Sea
TURKEY
CYPRUS 1960
MALTA 1964
SYRIA
LEBANON
PALESTINE 1948
IRAQ
IRAN
MOROCCO
TUNISIA
WESTERN SAHARA
ALGERIA
LIBYA
EGYPT 1956
JORDAN 1946
KUWAIT 1961
UNITED ARAB EMIRATES 1971
SAUDI ARABIA
BAHRAIN 1971
QATAR 1971
OMAN 1971
MAURITANIA
MALI
NIGER
CHAD
SUDAN 1956
YEMEN ARAB REP
DEM. REP. OF YEMEN 1967
Aden 1967
SENEGAL
GAMBIA 1965
GUINEA-BISSAU
GUINEA
UPPER VOLTA
NIGERIA 1960
ETHIOPIA
BRITISH SOMALI-LAND 1960
SIERRA LEONE 1961
LIBERIA
IVORY COAST
TOGO
DAHOMEY
CAMEROON
CENTRAL AFRICAN REP.
UGANDA 1962
KENYA 1963
SOMALIA
GABON
CONGO
ZAÏRE
TANZANIA 1964
SEYCHELLES
ATLANTIC
ANGOLA
MALAWI 1964
ZAMBIA 1964
S.W. AFRICA (NAMIBIA) 1971
RHODESIA 1965
MOZAMBIQUE
MADAGASCAR
MAURITIUS 1968
OCEAN
BOTSWANA 1966
SOUTH AFRICA 1961 (REP.)
SWAZILAND 1968
LESOTHO 1966

British or British-protected territories, with
dates of independence or British withdrawal

unambiguous statement of Britain's military and financial
inability and above all lack of will, to retain possession of
distant lands by force. The process of decolonization gained in
momentum in the fifties, with territories in West and East
Africa and elsewhere receiving their independence, even Kenya
and Cyprus, where there were bloody engagements against
native nationalist forces. In southern Africa, the eventual break-
up of the Central African Federation in 1963 meant independence for Northern Rhodesia (Zambia) and Nyasaland (Malawi)
also. By the early 1960s, only a scattered handful of miscellaneous territories—British Honduras, the barren wastes of the
Falkland Islands, Gibraltar, Hong Kong, Aden, Fiji, and a few

other outposts—were still under direct British rule. There was little enough nostalgic hankering for the mystique of empire now. Empire Day disappeared from the calendar of state schools; Indian civil servants anonymously returned home; the king ceased to be Emperor of India. Then in October 1956, the Prime Minister of the time, Anthony Eden, astonishingly engaged in covert moves with the French and the Israelis to invade the Suez Canal Zone, after the Egyptians had declared that that crucial waterway was henceforth to be nationalized. World opinion turned against Britain, even in the United States. Sterling was threatened; oil supplies dried up; the British troops withdrew ignominiously, censured by the United Nations.

There were few signs of prolonged public anger; the voices of the older imperialism were relatively muted. In the 1959 general election, the Conservatives fought, and comfortably won, on the basis of domestic prosperity—'You've never had it so good', in the argot of Macmillan. On the other hand, the American politician, Daniel Moynihan, could write of the new prestige of Britain in the Afro-Asian Third World for having liberated so large a proportion of the world's population without the bitterness of the French in Algeria, the Dutch in Indonesia, or the Belgians in the Congo. A world that had once listened to the liberal nostrums of Bentham and Ricardo, Mill and Gladstone, now hearkened to the social democratic creed proclaimed by Laski and Tawney of the London School of Economics, the *New Statesman*, and (even in opposition) the Labour Party.

In its post-imperial phase, Britain became a more introspective power, one whose role in world affairs was uncertain. As the Commonwealth connection became more ceremonial —though with important practical aspects like the imperial preferences for Commonwealth products such as butter and meat—the relationship with America, bitter-sweet in many ways, loomed ever larger. From 1949 the United States and Britain were bound together, strategically and geo-politically, in NATO. Another organization SEATO, for South-East Asia, followed on shortly. Thereafter, British and American policies marched closely together, whether a Conservative or a Labour government was in power. The British prided themselves that this meant an equal 'special relationship' between the English-speaking peoples. It is clear, however, that in practice this relationship involved Britain striving desperately to maintain an illusory posture of independence. In the Korean War, in dealings with Communist China (other than its formal recognition), in the Middle East, above all in Europe in the face of Russian threats, British and American policies were similar, if not identical. A rare attempt at rebellion such as the British involvement in the Suez operation in 1956 was quickly snuffed out. The

Nassau agreements led to defence and economic dependence on the United States being more pronounced than ever.

Nearer home, there were attempts from 1947 onwards to form a political and economic union of Western Europe. From the dawn of this idea just after the war, British governments were suspicious, if not openly hostile. They cited the Commonwealth connection, the special relationship with the United States, the distinctiveness of the British constitutional and legal system, the autonomy of British socialist planning. More powerfully, most British people regarded other Western Europeans as incomprehensible aliens, with few natural ties linking them across the English Channel. The first British attempt to join the European Common Market was rebuffed by President de Gaulle of France in 1963; years passed before another effort was made. It cannot be said that the British showed any overwhelming sense of grief at this failure to be admitted to an alien institution which would mean dearer food and a threat to national sovereignty. The Euro-enthusiasts were swimming against the clear tide of public opinion.

In this self-contained, somewhat insular, society, the general pattern was set by consumer-led affluence. Beneath the surface, economists, the new soothsayers of the age, detected slow rates of growth and falling productivity. Sociologists unearthed deep inequalities and class divisions which prevented the modernizing of a 'stagnant society'. Attitudes to British institutions and conventions were maked by an overpowering complacency. For the British, life seemed now distinctly better. A falling birth-rate meant smaller and more affluent households. Homes were better furnished. Families increasingly had cars; they could buy their homes on cheap mortgages; they managed each summer a decent holiday abroad in Spain, France, or Italy. Nor were these growing delights confined to the semi-detached middle class in the suburbs. Working-class people also enjoyed airlifted package holidays to the sunny Mediterranean coast, and revelled, in pubs, clubs, and elsewhere, in the freedom of choice afforded by higher wages and shorter working hours. The working-class young became a favourite target for sociological analysis and conventional head-shaking, with their more eccentric life-styles and a more expansive pop culture. A sporting hero such as the long-haired Northern Ireland and Manchester United footballer, George Best, suggested very different values from those of Jack Hobbs in the twenties. The musical breakthrough effected in the early 1960s by the Beatles, a group of Liverpudlian youths, made Britain the harbinger of the supposedly 'permissive' society, in which drink and drugs were freely available, skirts spectacularly shorter, sexual restraint much less in evidence. England's football World Cup victory in 1966 added an aura of patriotism to the new aggressiveness of the young.

In addition, middle-class reformers pioneered other social changes, assisted by the hedonistic outlook of a Prime Minister such as Harold Macmillan, and the civilized tolerance of a Labour Home Secretary, Roy Jenkins. Sexual offences, homosexual and otherwise, were less liable to the rigours of the law. Abortion, along with the pill and other easily obtainable contraceptives, offered scope for endless sexual indulgence; there were far more divorces, and one-parent families. The youth cult seemed for a time to be sweeping the land, allegedly fostered by President Kennedy's 'New Frontier' in America. In particular, a variety of cultures mingled in British universities. Here a growing number of uprooted working-class students merged with more aggressive middle-class contemporaries to fortify the appeal to youth with the protection of mere numbers. Many new universities sprang up in the ten years after 1963, while older universities were much expanded. 'More meant worse' complained some critics. Others countered that British potential was scarcely being exploited when only 5 per cent of the relevant age-group went on to higher education of any kind. Since the basic problems of subsistence were apparently being resolved by the economics of abundance, the articulate university young could turn their energies to new crusades.

The Campaign for Nuclear Disarmament in the later fifties owed much to the idealism of the middle-class young. For a time, it threatened to undermine the Labour Party as a potential party of government. Later in the sixties, the same kind of passion flowed into protest against the American war in Vietnam. Student rebellion, familiar abroad in Berkeley or the Sorbonne, briefly flared up in British campuses, and then equally mysteriously, petered out.

These movements had wider implications. Beneath the veneer of public contentment, there were in reality a variety of divisive forces that were deeply entrenched. A wide range of different groups were, in the period of Harold Wilson's first premiership (1964–70), exploding into revolt. The young, as has been seen, were finding the values of consumerism and conformism unappealing in a world whose ecology was being disturbed and whose very existence was threatened by weapons of unimaginable horror. Elsewhere, young people in Wales and Scotland generated a tide of nationalist protest, more familiar in the Basque regions of Spain or in French Quebec. Wales and Scotland had not fully enjoyed the economic growth of the 1950s. Their national aspirations were hardly fulfilled by such formal institutions as the Secretaries of State created for Scotland and much later (in 1964) for Wales. Scottish nationalists complained, with justice, that the very title of Elizabeth II was a misnomer in their country. In Wales, there was the added theme of an ancient language and culture threatened with extinction in the unequal battle against anglicized 'admass' culture. Victory for a Welsh Nationalist at Carmarthen in a by-election in 1966 was followed by renewed civil disobedience (and a few bombing attempts) on behalf of the Welsh language. In Scotland, the Nationalists captured the Hamilton seat, and several local authorities; a new anti-English mood seemed to be sweeping Highlands and Lowlands alike. Less constitutional or placid were the demands of the black or brown minorities, over a million of whom had migrated to Britain from India, Pakistan, West Africa, and the West Indies since

1950. In addition to dilapidated housing and racial discrimination in employment and (sometimes) at the hands of the police, there was the added hazard of racial bigotry in older urban areas. This was fanned by the inflammatory rhetoric of a maverick right-wing Cassandra, Enoch Powell. 'Rivers of blood' were forecast in British cities on the lines of the race riots of the United States.

More disturbing still, in Northern Ireland, an artificial state kept in being by the control of the Protestant majority from 1920 onwards was in disarray. A powerful civil rights movement arose on behalf of the Roman Catholic (and usually nationalist) minority. But, in practice, attempts to maintain religious and racial harmony clearly broke down. Troops were moved into Belfast and Londonderry to preserve order. An alarming wave of bombing attacks in English cities signified that the IRA and Sinn Fein were taking the age-old struggle of Irish nationalism into a new and sinister phase. In the later sixties, with minorities on the march from Brixton to Belfast, liberal consensual Britain seemed to be breaking down, as it had almost done in 1910–14.

Hitherto the social fabric had been kept intact, at least in part, because of high and advancing living standards for the population as a whole. But clear evidence mounted up in the 1960s that increasing economic pressures were adding to the new social tensions. Britain lurched in that miserable decade from one financial expedient to another, with frequent balance of payments crises and many runs on sterling. Devaluation of the pound in 1967 did not produce any lasting remedy. Inflation began to rise significantly, especially in the early 1970s when a Conservative government under Edward Heath recklessly expanded the money supply, a misguided version of Keynesianism. All the predictions of Keynesian economists were now overturned as rising inflation was accompanied by a growing toll of unemployment as well. At first this was confined to the older industrial regions of the north-east, Scotland, and South Wales. The rise of nationalism in the last two was much associated with the closure of collieries and factories and the laying off of labour. But by 1973 it was clear that the economic problems of Britain were having far more general consequences. The nation's capacity to generate wealth, along with its share of world trade and production, were in serious, perhaps terminal, decline. Britain seemed to have replaced Turkey as the legendary 'sick man of Europe'. In retaliation for declining living standards, the unions replied with collective industrial power. Strikes mounted up, most acutely in the case of the coal mines. A national miners' strike was called in February 1972 and was wholly successful. The Heath government experienced the full extent of the miners' ability to disrupt national production and energy supplies, despite all the contraction of the coal industry since the 1950s. Another miners' strike in February 1974 saw the government call an election on the theme of: 'Who governs Britain?' The answer was a small swing to Labour and the government duly fell. The miners again won all their demands and their former place high in the wages table. This background of a widening mood of protest, a reluctance to accept traditional sanctions and disciplines, institutional power from the unions thrust against a declining productive base— these formed the ominous backcloth as Britain emerged from its brief, heady acquaintance with 'affluence' to confront the unfamiliar challenges of a new international order.

From the Seventies to the Nineties

In the nineteen-seventies, Britain offered a permanent, painful case for macro-economic and sociological treatment. Its economic decline continued, comparatively in relation to almost all other developed nations, and even in absolute terms compared with earlier production levels. It was much aggravated by the dramatic change in the energy situation in 1973–4 as a result of which Britain and other Western nations suffered a fourfold increase in the price of Middle East oil. This gave new impetus to Britain's own major development in this decade, the exploitation of the oil reserves in the North Sea, and of North Sea natural gas also. With nuclear power stations and hydro-electric schemes, as well as abundant supplies of coal, Britain was in many ways far better prepared to confront these new difficulties than many of its competitors. But the huge rise in the price of oil inevitably fuelled inflation on a scale unknown since 1919. It was reinforced by trade union pressure for enormous wage increases of anything up to 30 per cent until late 1975. British inflation continued to run at a historically high level, reaching over 20 per cent for a time in 1980, before it sank in 1982–3 to a more manageable figure of less than half that amount. Thereafter, curbs on the money supply, aided by a slow-down in wage increases and a relative fall in the real price of many commodities, saw the inflation rate subside to around 4 per cent by the autumn of 1987. With surging price rises and pressure from wage and other unit costs, unemployment re-emerged as the major domestic scourge. By 1980 it was over two million, a total unknown since the thirties. With government investment and the money supply curtailed, unemployment had advanced to well over three million by the spring of 1983. It remained at that alarming total for the next three years, even creeping up somewhat, until some renewed economic growth saw a slight fall to below three million in 1987. There seemed to be a deep rot at the heart of the economy, with hundreds of thousands, many of them teenagers or other young people, doomed to perhaps years on national assistance, while public welfare services were steadily curtailed. There was evidence of decline elsewhere as well. Although the population continued to increase, from over 50 million in 1951 to over 56 million in 1981, it was noted that there was actually a fall in the period 1975–8. The birth-rate fell sharply during the recession, while a larger proportion of the population were elderly, placing strains on the social services and necessarily reliant on the wealth created by the able-bodied still in employment.

The outcome was most disruptive for the social fabric. An

initial period of runaway inflation in 1974–5 was stemmed by a period of an uneasy so-called 'social contract' with the unions, negotiated by the Labour governments of Wilson and then Callaghan in 1975–8. Unions agreed to moderate their wage demands in return for specified government policies geared to their needs, and especially to job protection. There were no serious strikes thereafter, until the so-called 'winter of discontent' in 1978–9, when a rash of strikes by public service workers, including even council grave-diggers, helped to ensure a Conservative election victory. Thereafter, the unions continued to be assertive in 'right-to-work' demonstrations in protest at cuts in public spending and the high rate of unemployment. Not only traditionally vulnerable areas such as Scotland, Merseyside, and the north-east but even once thriving regions such as the West Midlands showed rates of joblessness amounting to over 20 per cent. In the steel industry, mighty plants like Consett, Shotton, and Corby were closed down for ever. More indirectly, the quality of life was impoverished by declining investment in health and educational services (including the universities) and by reduced expenditure on art and the environment. Britain now provided a classic example of the post-Keynesian phenomenon of 'stagflation', with industrial recession and high inflation at one and the same time.

These economic pressures led to severe strains being placed on the stability of society in the seventies. They fuelled other social, communal, or ethnic tensions already much in evidence. The most disturbing case was still Northern Ireland where deep-seated racial and religious animosities between Protestants and Roman Catholics were aggravated by the most acute rate of unemployment in the United Kingdom. Throughout the seventies, the state of Northern Ireland became more and more alarming. The success of the civil rights movement dislodged the old Unionist ascendancy; the Stormont assembly was wound up in 1972 in favour of direct rule by Westminster. But renewed violence by the IRA was paralleled by the aggressive anti-Papist demagogy of the Reverend Ian Paisley. The end of

Stormont certainly brought communal peace no nearer. Troops continued to patrol the Bogside and the Falls Road. There were tense border incidents between Ulster and the Irish Republic to the south, from where the IRA derived funds and weapons. On occasion, the endemic violence of Northern Ireland stretched across the sea in the form of terrifying bomb attacks on English cities, and even assassinations of politicians. The Queen's relative, the distinguished admiral and statesman, Lord Mountbatten, was murdered, blown up on his yacht by an IRA bomb. A new effort to involve the Dublin government in the affairs of Northern Ireland directly, the first since 1922, came with the Anglo-Irish Hillsborough Agreement, concluded between the British Prime Minister, Mrs Thatcher, and the Irish Fine Gael Premier, Dr Garret FitzGerald, in November 1985. But this led to bitter protests from Unionists in Ulster who then boycotted Westminster. A genuine all-Ireland spirit of unity in that unhappy island remained far off. The age-old racial feuds of Ireland were not yet pacified. Repeated acts of violence, including an abortive mortar attack by the IRA on 10 Downing Street in February 1991, drove the point home for the general public.

Other tensions of the period were less violent but equally disturbing. Scottish and Welsh nationalists continued to express themselves though usually in constitutional form. After the failure of 'devolution' measures in 1979, Celtic nationalism seemed to be in retreat, but in Wales especially there continued to be much political and cutural conflict. The defence of the Welsh language still attracted much passionate loyalty, and even threats of fasts unto death by angry patriots. Englishmen who owned a 'second home' in the Welsh countryside sometimes found it burned down by local incendiarists. Pressure for governmental devolution remained powerful in Scotland, fuelled by the relative decline of its economic base in the 1980s. Wales and Scotland, however, remained, on balance, peaceful societies, less torn apart by nationalist anguish than their Celtic neighbour across the sea. More alarming were the troubles afflicting the large black community, much of it resident in poor, dilapidated ghetto areas in large cities. There were sporadic troubles in the Notting Hill area of London and the St. Paul's district of Bristol. In the summer of 1981 it seemed for a time that Britain was experiencing the full horrors of race riots on the American pattern, as black youths in the Toxteth area of Liverpool and the Brixton district of south London engaged in prolonged rioting, all faithfully recorded (and perhaps whipped up) by television reporting. Another violent flare-up saw disturbances on the Broadwater Farm housing estate in Tottenham, north London, and the murder of a policeman there by black youths. A lack of trust between the immigrant community and the police force was one notable aspect of these events. But, with unemployment especially serious for young blacks and a pervasive background of discrimination in jobs, housing, and social opportunity, the relations between the races was a mounting cause for concern and alarm.

Other troubles piled up. Some examples of trade union protest, for instance the demonstrations against the Grunwick works in north London, seemed to go far beyond the usual limits of industrial protest in the intimidation that characterized them. Football matches and other sporting occasions were scarred by mindless violence by teenage spectators. Britain's traditional stability appeared, therefore, increasingly under fire from many sources. An American congressman gloomily observed that Britain was becoming as 'ungovernable as Chile', an alarming parallel for Americans. This proved to be an absurd exaggeration. Few societies would have survived high unemployment, rising inflation, and public retrenchment with as much equanimity as did the British. Despite evidence of hallowed institutions being treated with less than their historic respect—Oxford University being subjected to 'sit-ins'; police, judges, Church leaders (and football referees) failing to sustain their former authority; even members of the royal family being subjected to public criticism or harassment—the broad fabric of institutional and civic life held firm. But, without doubt, the points of friction and potential dissolution were so numerous that age-old sanctions and restraints would have to be re-examined and re-defined for British civilization to survive at all.

During this period of some turmoil, Britain's view of the outside world underwent a phase of introspection. In practice, a deep psychology of insularity dictated popular attitudes, as it had frequently done since 1918. The formal alliance with the Americans in NATO continued, but attracted little passionate commitment. Indeed, the revival in the late 1970s of the Campaign for Nuclear Disarmament, a singularly peaceful form of protest, suggested that the dependence of this alliance on a mounting arsenal of nuclear weapons of a quite horrific kind aroused much public disquiet. The proposed Cruise missiles aroused still more. After much diplomatic infighting, Britain entered the European Common Market in 1973. A unique referendum in 1975 saw a large majority, almost two-thirds in all, recording its support for British membership. But 'Europe' attracted affection largely in non-political contexts. Continental package holidays, the popularity of Continental cars and food products, European football matches did not make the British love their neighbours across the Channel any more fervently. British attitudes towards the Common Market continued after 1975 to be governed by sullen hostility; opinion polls recorded consistent opposition to membership of the EEC. In any case, an organization which consisted largely of a massive, anonymous, bureaucratic juggernaut, with scant democratic constraint, located far away in Brussels and Strasbourg could hardly win public love in as independent a nation as Britain. The linking of the Common Market with higher food prices, butter mountains, wine lakes and the like, was widely condemned, inevitably so by a people which had known a policy of cheap food since the repeal of the Corn Laws in 1846. The British were reluctant Europeans as they were reluctant Atlanticists.

On the other hand, there were signs by the later eighties that the British were becoming more reconciled to the fact that membership of the European community and that anti-Europeanism was diminishing. By the June 1987 general election, the Labour Party no longer proposed to negotiate British withdrawal from the EEC, especially since the latter now included socialist governments in France, Spain and Greece. The agreement concluded in 1986 between Mrs Thatcher and President Mitterrand of France to complete a high-speed rail tunnel under the English Channel to link Britain and France, a tunnel due to be operating in 1993, was a dramatic indication of at least a partial retreat from British isolationism. Britain agreed to enter the European Single Market in 1992, a momentous change. Finally, after much internal argument in her Cabinet, Mrs Thatcher was forced to enter the European Exchange Rate Mechanism in October 1990. Nevertheless the economic and political relationship with Europe remained a deeply divisive issue at several levels of the Conservative party and government. It played a major part in Mrs Thatcher being forced to step down as Prime Minister in November 1990, after over eleven years in power.

Commonwealth sentiment still retained some force with the Queen as its figurehead. Yet the Commonwealth ties were becoming more and more intangible, too. Whether in the forms of coloured immigrants into British cities or arguments over how to respond to *apartheid* in South Africa, they could produce friction rather than goodwill. Meanwhile the agreement with China in 1989 to withdraw the British presence in Hong Kong eight years later confirmed the irreversible retreat from a world role.

The withdrawal from empire continued apace with little public resentment. Economic and military weakness dictated a policy of controlled retreat. The most difficult surviving problem was that of Southern Rhodesia, where a racial holocaust was threatened in a land adjacent to South Africa with its apartheid system. In a dramatic reversal, Mrs Thatcher's Conservative government granted total self-government to Rhodesia (renamed Zimbabwe) in December 1979; the protests of white settlers were ignored. Parliament and public greeted this imperial retreat with a fanfare of acclamation. The spirit of Kipling and Rhodes had finally been exorcized. It seemed unlikely that empire would disturb the British psyche any further.

Then, quite unexpectedly, the distant barren outpost of the Falkland Islands was invaded by the Argentines in late March 1982. The British government responded vigorously in the face of a huge public outcry. The two remaining aircraft-carriers and dozens of other war vessels, many fighter planes, and 10,000 troops were assembled in a task force and dispatched 8,000 miles away to the stormy seas of the South Atlantic. In a swift and successful campaign, the islands were soon recaptured; the Union Jack again flew in Port Stanley on 14 June. The Falklands War was immensely popular; dissidents, CND or otherwise, were unable to gain a fair hearing. At the same time, it seemed most improbable that a war to retain these distant and almost valueless outposts, scarcely known to British people before the fighting began other than from postage stamps, would encourage a revived mystique of imperial grandeur. There was no more popular anxiety to commit naval strength or financial resources to the South Atlantic after the war than there had been before. What the Falklands episode possibly did was to confirm a rising tide of impatient insularity amongst the British people. In the face of international scepticism, Britain could still display great-power status, and demonstrate its military, naval, and technological superiority over a Fascist dictatorship such as the Argentine republic. National pride was refurbished.

But the jingoism of the Falklands petered out almost as soon as it began. Britain returned to the familiar domestic scene of strikes, economic decline, and social discontent, exemplified by a bitter miners' strike from March 1984 which lasted a whole year. There were violent clashes between the police and miners' pickets. However, the National Union of Mineworkers was itself divided, with important Midlands' coalfields continuing to work, and the result was a profound defeat for the NUM and the closure of many more pits. The power of the miners to coerce a British government into submission, a major feature of history and folklore since the First World War, was no longer apparent when coal was less essential to Britain's energy supplies, and with oil, gas, electricity, and nuclear power readily available. The miners' strike, however, was followed by a series of strikes by white-collar and public service workers, notably a lengthy dispute by Britain's schoolteachers which led to much disruption in schools in England and Wales in 1985–7.

The problems of the early eighties were intensified by a Conservative government under Mrs Thatcher which seemed to be the most right-wing that Britain had known in the twentieth century. At the same time, the Labour Party, with Tony Benn spearheading a grass-roots movement towards fundamentalist socialism, appeared to be moving equally far to the left. Consensus seemed to have disappeared. Pedants quoted W. B. Yeats to the effect that 'the best lacked all conviction and the worst were full of passionate intensity'. Some found solace in a new political party formed by dissident right-wing members of the Labour Party; this was the 'Social Democratic Party', committed to Keynes-style economic centrism, to an incomes policy, Europeanism, and the nuclear deterrent. Remarkably, despite much fatalism about the economy, the June 1983 general election provided an immense triumph for Mrs Thatcher and the Conservatives. They captured 397 seats, as against 209 for a visibly declining Labour Party, 17 for the Liberals, and only 6 for the SDP. But renewed fears for moderate middle-ground opinion being swept away in the maelstrom were somewhat assuaged by other, more hopeful developments. The economic changes in the country were not without compensation. In part, they were the result of a beneficial change in the national economy, with Britain becoming self-sufficient in North Sea oil, and thus in a unique position of strength in its energy base. The balance of payments suddenly moved (until 1986) into a large and continuing surplus. This also meant that the dominance of manufacturing industry in the British economy would be far less paramount henceforth. Certainly the technological wonders of oil, electronics, and aerospace, of Concorde, the Humber Bridge, the High-Speed Train, the Channel Tunnel, and the computerized microchip age suggested that the native reserves of innovation and scientific ingenuity had not run dry.

In the mid-eighties, there were some signs, too, that these developments were helping to generate a renewal of affluence, at least for southern England, parts of the Midlands, and East Anglia, the last an area of particular growth. The British economy began to advance rapidly and reached a rate of 4 per cent growth in early 1987, assisted by the fall in the value of the pound and of some imported commodities. It was noticeable that this advance rested less on Britain's traditional strength in manufacturing, which continued to lag far below pre-1970 levels of production, than on credit, investment, and a consumer boom. A notable event here was the so-called 'Big Bang' in the City of London 27 October 1986, which replaced the age-old spectacle of jobbers milling on the Stock Exchange floor with an almost invisible, highly sophisticated computer-based network for dealers. This reflected the new internationalism of the capital market. It also contributed, incidentally, to repairing decades of neglect and dereliction in adjacent areas of London's East End. The social phenomenon of the 'yuppy' (young upwardly-mobile professional), a money-making youth engaged in stock-broking, investment or merchant banking, was widely discussed. For many British citizens, life suddenly appeared easier after the crises of the seventies and early eighties. Home ownership continued to spread· until by the end of 1987, two-thirds of the population owned their own home. Share-owning also became more widespread. The government's policy of 'privatizing' state-owned enterprises such as the telecommunications system, British Gas, Britoil and the airports (with water and electricity to follow at the end of the decade) helped towards this last end. Conversely, the trade unions appeared to be declining in public esteem and even more in membership which slumped from around 13 million in 1980 to 9 million in 1987.

The land was not proving to be culturally barren or intellectually unadventurous at this time. British novelists and dramatists remained remarkably creative. Several leading British architects achieved international renown. The British musical scene was never more flourishing than in the 1980s with London plausibly claimed to be the musical capital of the world, and important new orchestral and operatic developments in Leeds, Cardiff, and elsewhere. British weekly literary periodicals remained of high quality. The BBC remained a major communications agency, though much distracted by disputes with the Thatcher government, and weakened by falling morale and revenue. Universities still maintained a flow of creative achievement in the arts and pure and applied science, including medicine, despite a policy of severe government cuts imposed from 1981 onwards. One American commentator, Bernard Nossiter, had even claimed in the late seventies, that the apparent economic rundown and unemployment in Britain masked something more positive—a deliberately creative use of leisure in which the British middle and skilled working class rebelled against the norms of ever-increasing mass production, and opted for greater freedom from the drudgery of automated labour. This view was probably too optimistic and ignored long-held traditions in antique working practices and managerial inertia which held the economy, and to some extent society, in thrall. In addition, the material base on which British culture rested was threatened by a renewed failure in technological innovation and enterprise. The problems of British universities and research institutes aroused great concern in the mid-eighties, with the 'brain drain' of gifted young scientists across the Atlantic. Two hundred years after the dawn of the Industrial Revolution, the British were still strangely reluctant to modernize and promote their scientific genius. Yet, despite this glaring weakness, British talents were not necessarily unequipped to cope with the new stresses of sociological upheaval and relative industrial weakness any more than with the burdens of commercial leadership and international power in past centuries.

These and other developments helped give a new lease of life to the Conservative government of Mrs Margaret Thatcher. In the

June 1987 general election, despite a vigorous Labour campaign under a new leader, Neil Kinnock, the Conservatives again won an easy victory with 375 seats as against 229 for Labour and only 22 for a flagging and disintegrating Liberal/Social Democrat Alliance. Mrs Thatcher thus became the first Prime Minister since Lord Liverpool in 1812–27 to win three successive general elections, an extraordinary achievement. The Conservatives made much in the campaign for their claims to have restored national prosperity, and also to be reliable protectors of national security. Labour's policy of unilateral nuclear disarmament did not command wide support. On the other hand, the regional gulf in Britain revealed by the election returns was very plain. The sweeping Conservative gains came in the South and the Midlands. They lost ground in the industrial cities of the North; there was a 5 per cent swing to Labour in Wales; and a 7.5 per cent swing in Scotland. There was much talk of a basic social divide in the land, between an increasingly prosperous and complacent South, and a decaying, declining North, with endemic unemployment, urban dereliction, and collapsing public services. The 'two nations', described in Disraeli's novels in the 1840s, were still much in evidence well over a century later.

Britain in the 1980s manifested a remarkable skein of elements of dissolution and stability, in fragile coexistence. The forces of disruption were evident enough. There were physical reminders in the troubles in Northern Ireland, in the industrial world, and in the black ghettos in the cities. There was the new challenge to the political consensus posed in their various guises by the neo-Marxist Labour left headed by Benn, by the racialist perversities of the quasi-Fascist National Front, perhaps by the patrician élitism displayed at times by some Social Democrats. Traditional relationships—the young towards their parents, 'feminist' wives towards their husbands, workers towards their employers and union leaders, students towards their teachers, citizens towards the custodians of law and order—seemed to be in flux. *Is Britain Dying?* was one evocative book title in 1979. British stability was too often expressed, by contrast, in an almost religious reverence for ancient forms and ancestor worship, as in the veneration of the royal family, or the ambiguous notion of 'heritage', which often entailed a distinctly selective and sentimental reading of British history.

Public instability was markedly reinforced by the disarray into which Mrs Thatcher's government lurched after the 1987 general election. For most of the decade, with its creed of monetarism, privatization, and the primacy of market forces; with its attacks on institutions such as the Church, the universities, and local government; with the almost invincible personal ascendancy of the Prime Minister herself, 'Thatcherism' seemed triumphant. But over the next three years it ran into severe difficulties. At home, some of its more radical proposals met with major opposition. Attempts to introduce market forces into education and even more into the National Health Service aroused great public anger. A proposal to abolish the system of household rates with a community charge (or 'poll tax') led to an upsurge of revolt across the nation. After all, freeborn Englishmen, headed by Wat Tyler, had rebelled against a poll tax as early as 1381 and the memory of it remained in popular legend. Most serious of all, the apparent revival in the economy began to lose credibility. The tax-cutting policy of the Chancellor, Nigel Lawson, was now seen to have led to a huge balance of payments deficit, at £20 billion the worst figure on record. Unemployment rose sharply and the pound came under pressure. Worse still, the conquest of inflation, the government's main boast, was now threatened by a consumer-credit and spending boom. Bank rate soared to 15 per cent, and the impact was felt by every mortgaged home-owner in the land. To make matters worse, the Chancellor, Nigel Lawson, locked in bitter argument with the Prime Minister over European policy, resigned. Mrs Thatcher herself now became increasingly unpopular. Her intensely personal, imperious style of leadership now seemed more of a liability. Her reputation for 'strength' in foreign affairs, dating from the Falklands War, also seemed less credible, especially with repeated rows over monetary union with our European partners. At the same time, the Labour Party, responding to Neil Kinnock's 'new realism' became increasingly moderate and therefore more electable. It dropped its commitment to mass nationalization and unilateral nuclear disarmament, and its hostility towards Europe, and turned on the hard-left Bennite remnants in the process. In the summer of 1990 it seemed that a sea change in British politics might be at hand.

In the autumn, the transformation duly occurred. Faced with Cabinet resignations, by-election losses, and difficulties over Europe and the economy, Mrs Thatcher seemed beleaguered as never before. She was then challenged for the party leadership (in effect, for the premiership) in November by Michael Heseltine, one of the many former Cabinet colleagues who had resigned from her government. Although Mrs Thatcher won the first ballot (204 votes to Heseltine's 152), the opposition to her within her party was sufficient to force her to resign. Like Lloyd George in 1922 and Neville Chamberlain in 1940, it was the Tory backbenchers, not the voters, who brought her down. In the second ballot, the victor was John Major, the little-known Chancellor of the Exchequer, and a man of apparently moderate views. He thus became Prime Minister, to guide the nation through the transition from the storms of 'Thatcherism' to a more consensual social and political order. At first, the Conservatives' disarray appeared to subside. The involvement of British forces in the Gulf War in February 1991, when British troops and jet fighters were prominent in assisting the Americans and other 'coalition' forces to drive Saddam Hussein's Iraqi armies out of occupied Kuwait, helped in the government's popularity for a brief period. But there was no 'Falklands factor' on this occasion to boost the Tory cause. On the contrary, the poll tax (finally disposed of in the spring of 1991), Europe, and other issues continued to haunt the government. Most serious of all, the economy showed signs of the kind of deep recession that had repeatedly afflicted the country over the past seventy years. High inflation and sagging production were now accompanied by rising unemployment which even took its toll of City 'yuppies' in the Tory heartlands. Like Wilson and Heath before him, John

Major was the hapless witness of simultaneous signs of national weakness at home and abroad. Northern Ireland was as intractable as ever; separatism in Scotland was gaining momentum. Public expectations about future national progress were muted.

The turbulence, however, seemed not incapable of control. Comparatively, in a violent century, Britain still remained a peaceful country, in which ancient institutions and norms commanded respect and adherence. Indeed, in some ways, the experimentalism of the 'permissive' years of the sixties was being followed by a new passion for traditional standards and values, commitment to a job, to more conventional forms of sexual experience, to family life, to a kind of patriotism. Conservative politicians tried to stimulate popular enthusiasm for what were claimed to be Victorian values. Even religious life showed some renewed vitality. In the turmoil of the eighties, Britain remained far from ungovernable. There was striking evidence from opinion polls which recorded, in the face of all the evidence and the processed gloom of the news media, a popular commitment to British life and an enthusiasm for one's country, rare in the Western world. Divisions were capable of being bridged in the light of a prevailing attachment to places, traditions, and myths. The more ceremonial aspects, such as the enthusiasm for the Crown, masked a more fundamental kind of commitment, to which West Indian and other newer immigrant citizens could also respond.

The truth was, perhaps, that Britain in the years from 1914 to 1991 had not changed all that fundamentally. Despite two world wars, the mass unemployment of the thirties, and the social turmoil of the seventies, the face of Great Britain, like Snowdonia or Thomas Hardy's Egdon Heath, might show surface changes of light or pattern; but the underlying geology remained the same. In 1991, as in 1914, the British retained a profound, non-exclusive sense of place. A loyalty to London or 'the North' or East Anglia or Cornwall, to the separate nationalities of Wales and Scotland, was still a living reality. The population remained intensely various, distinct, individual.

More parochially, there was the rich, voluntary involvement in village or small-town life, often translated in surprising forms into larger conurbations as well. Britain in the 1990s remained a relatively neighbourly society. Most powerfully of all, the British constantly expressed a deep sense of their history. Even in the turbulence of the later twentieth century, an awareness of the past came through as variously as in old cathedral cities, or in the Durham Miners' Gala or the Welsh national *eisteddfod* or the Highland games. The monarchy and Parliament embodied this sense of history; so, too, more painfully, did the sense of resolve generated by the crisis of war or external threat. In the mass media, historical or other documentary productions on television or film revived the mystique of ancient identity, just as the broadcasting services were powerful in the self-awareness of the Scots, Welsh, and Northern Irish. In spite of decades of almost unbearable upheaval, Britain remained an organic, closely knit society, capable of self-renewal. Its very forms of native protest often testified to an innate tolerance and gentleness, a respect for individuality and eccentricity, a rejection of coercion and uniformity. The 'Liberty tree' was being nurtured in 1991, as with the Levellers or Tom Paine. In the later twentieth century, as in times of greater pomp, power, and prosperity in the past, the values of being British could still be affirmed and sustained. So might they be again, in centuries yet to unfold.

FURTHER READING

1. THE LIBERAL AGE

GENERAL SURVEYS

Asa Briggs, *The Age of Improvement* (London, 1959), a good political and social survey of the period up to 1867.

D. Read, *England 1868–1914* (London, 1979), a competent, detailed survey.

Geoffrey Best, *Mid-Victorian Britain 1851–1870* (London, 1971), a predominantly social account.

R. C. K. Ensor, *England, 1870–1914* (Oxford, 1936, often reprinted), still has material and analysis of value.

E. Halévy, *History of the English People in the Nineteenth Century*, vols. 5 (*Imperialism and the Rise of Labour, 1895–1905*) and 6 (*The Rule of Democracy, 1905–1914*) (rev. edn. London, 1951–2), a classic account, based on contemporary published material, which still holds its own.

ECONOMIC HISTORY

P. Mathias, *The First Industrial Nation* (2nd rev. edn. London, 1983), a clear and concise account.

E. Hobsbawm, *Industry and Empire* (London, 1968), an incisive argument, stressing the socio-economic shift from industry to commerce.

D. Landes, *The Unbound Prometheus. Technological Change, 1750 to the Present* (Cambridge, 1969), the relationship of technology to industry.

SOCIAL LIFE

H. J. Dyos and M. Wolff (eds.), *The Victorian City*, 2 vols. (London, 1973), splendidly comprehensive illustrations.

G. Mingay (ed.), *The Victorian Countryside*, 2 vols. (London, 1981), the complementary work.

Robert Roberts, *The Classic Slum* (London, 1971), childhood in Salford.

Florence, Lady Bell, *At the Works* (London, 1911 edn.), vivid and acute analysis of social life in Middlesbrough.

Flora Thompson, *Lark Rise to Candleford* (Oxford, 1945, often reprinted), the Oxfordshire countryside in decline.

Owen Chadwick, *The Victorian Church*, 2 vols. (3rd edn. London, 1971), a powerful survey, rather favourable to Anglicanism.

Asa Briggs, *Victorian Cities* (London, 1963), and *Victorian People* (2nd edn. London, 1965), stimulating essays.

The Batsford series, *Victorian and Edwardian Life* in photographs (many vols. by city and county) is excellent; an important source.

V. A. C. Gatrell, B. Lenman, and G. Parker, *Crime and the Law: the Social History of Crime in Western Europe since 1500* (London, 1980).

POLITICAL LIFE

John Vincent, *The Formation of the Liberal Party, 1857–1868* (London, 1966), a brilliant if sometimes excessively paradoxical analysis.

Martin Pugh, *The Making of Modern British Politics 1867–1939* (London, 1982), an intelligent synthesis of recent research.

Robert Blake, *Disraeli* (London, 1966), the standard life.

H. C. G. Matthew, *Gladstone, 1809–1874* (Oxford, 1986).

Robert Blake, *The Conservative Party from Peel to Thatcher* (new edn. London, 1982), the party's fall and rise.

Paul Smith, *Disraelian Conservatism and Social Reform* (London, 1967), sets Conservative social policy in context.

Kenneth O. Morgan, *The Age of Lloyd George* (3rd edn. London, 1978), the best introduction to Liberalism after Gladstone.

José Harris, *Unemployment and Politics. A Study in English Social Policy 1886–1914* (Oxford, 1972; paperback 1984), a powerful critique of the early years of the welfare state.

Ross McKibbin, *The Evolution of the Labour Party, 1910–1924* (Oxford, 1974, paperback 1983), the standard work on the party's early years.

H. A. Clegg, A. Fox , and A. F. Thompson, *A History of British Trade Unions since 1889, vol. i. 1889–1910* (Oxford, 1964), indispensable account of the complexities of politics and industrial relations.

Henry Pelling, *Popular Politics and Society in Late Victorian Britain* (London, 1968), a volume of challenging reinterpretations.

A. Rosen, *Rise Up Women!* (London, 1974), places the suffragette movement in a searching light, with unflattering consequences.

Asa Briggs (ed.), *William Morris. Selected Writings and Designs* (London, 1962), gives a useful introduction to the art and craft movement.

SCOTLAND, IRELAND, WALES

F. S. L. Lyons, *Ireland since the Famine* (London, 1971), authoritative, from an Anglo-Irish viewpoint.

Kenneth O. Morgan, *Rebirth of a Nation: Wales 1880–1980* (Oxford and Cardiff, 1981), a sympathetic account from a moderately nationalist perspective.

Christopher Harvie, *Scotland and Nationalism* (London, 1977), lively and original.

IMPERIALISM

D. K. Fieldhouse, *The Colonial Empires* (London, 1966), an excellent survey.

R. Robinson and J. Gallagher, *Africa and the Victorians* (London, 1961), a bold thesis, arguing the superiority of strategic over economic motivation.

A. P. Thornton, *The Imperial Idea and its Enemies* (London, 1959), gives an elegant and witty account of the imperial debate.

A. J. P. Taylor, *The Troublemakers* (London, 1956, reprinted 1969), a heartfelt account of a tradition which failed.

Paul Kennedy, *The Realities behind Diplomacy* (London, 1981), offers a useful survey of the relationship of diplomacy to power.

A. J. P. Taylor, *The Struggle for Mastery in Europe, 1848–1918* (Oxford, 1954, often reprinted), a powerful analysis of the consequences of Germany's bid for power.

2. THE TWENTIETH CENTURY

GENERAL

T. O. Lloyd, *Empire to Welfare State. English History, 1906–1985* (3rd edn. Oxford, 1986), a good general survey.

C. L. Mowat, *Britain between the Wars* (London, 1955), excellent on social and economic themes.

Kenneth O. Morgan, *The People's Peace: British History; 1945–1990* (Oxford, 1992).

SOCIAL AND ECONOMIC

A. H. Halsey (ed.), *Trends in British Society since 1900* (London, 1972), comprehensive and factual.

Arthur Marwick, *The Deluge* (London, 1965), covers the effects of the First World War.

William Ashworth, *An Economic History of Britain, 1870–1939* (London, 1960).

Sidney Pollard, *The Development of the British Economy, 1914–1980* (3rd edn. London, 1983).

Alec Cairncross, *Years of Recovery: British Economic Policy, 1945–51* (London, 1985), a fine study of the Attlee years.

J. R. C. Dow, *The Management of the British Economic, 1945–60* (Cambridge 1964).

E. H. Phelps Brown, *The Growth of British Industrial Relations, 1906–14* (London, 1963).

——*The Origins of Trade Union Power* (Oxford, 1983).

Henry Pelling, *A History of British Trade Unionism* (2nd edn. London, 1971).

John Stevenson, *British Society, 1914–45* (London, 1984), good on the inter-war years.

G. C. Peden, *British Economic and Social Policy, Lloyd George to Margaret Thatcher* (Deddington, Oxon, 1985).

POLITICAL

Martin Pugh, *The Making of Modern British Politics, 1867–1939* (London, 1982), a useful survey for the student.

Samuel Beer, *Modern British Politics* (rev. edn. London, 1982), a stimulating thematic approach.

Robert Blake, *The Conservative Party from Peel to Thatcher* (new edn. London, 1985).

John Ramsden, *The Age of Balfour and Baldwin, 1902–40* (London, 1978).

Trevor Wilson, *The Downfall of the Liberal Party, 1914–1935* (London, 1966).

Ross McKibbin, *The Evolution of the Labour Party, 1910–1924* (Oxford, 1974; paperback 1983).

Cameron Hazlehurst, *Politicians at War, July 1914 to May 1915* (London, 1971).

Robert Skidelsky, *Politicians and the Slump* (London, 1968), the second Labour government.

Donald Cameron Watt, *How War Came* (London, 1989), a brilliant study of 1938–9.

Henry Pelling, *Britain and the second World War* (London, 1970).

Paul Addison, *The Road to 1945* (London, 1975).

Kenneth O. Morgan, *Labour in Power, 1945–1951* (Oxford, 1984).

—— *Labour People* (Oxford, 1992), studies of personalities from Hardie to Kinnock.

Dennis Kavanagh, *Thatcherism and British Politics* (Oxford, 1987).

David Marquand, *The Unprincipled Society* (London, 1988), a perceptive critique of the British political economy.

BIOGRAPHIES

Alan Bullock, *The Life and Times of Ernest Bevin*, 2 vols. (London, 1960, 1967).

—— *Ernest Bevin, Foreign Secretary 1945–1951* (London, 1983).

David Marquand, *Ramsay MacDonald* (London, 1977).

David Dilks, *Neville Chamberlain*, vol. 1 (Cambridge, 1984).

Kenneth Harris, *Attlee* (London, 1982).

Ben Pimlott, *Hugh Dalton* (London, 1985).

Robert Skidelsky, *John Maynard Keynes*, vol. 1 (London, 1983), a lively analysis of the years to 1919.

Christopher Hussey, *The Life of Sir Edwin Lutyens* (London, 1950).

Philip Williams, *Hugh Gaitskell* (London, 1979).

Bernard Crick, *George Orwell: a Life* (London, 1980).

Michael Holroyd, *Lytton Strachey*, 2 vols. (London 1967–8).

Hugo Young, *One of Us* (London, 1991).

SCOTLAND, IRELAND, WALES

Kenneth O. Morgan, *Rebirth of a Nation: Wales 1880–1980* (Oxford and Cardiff, 1981).

Christopher Harvie, *Scotland and Nationalism* (London, 1977).

—— *No Gods and Precious Few Heroes: Scotland, 1914–1980* (London, 1981).

F. S. L. Lyons, *Ireland since the Famine* (rev. edn. London, 1973), a definitive survey from the 1840s to the 1970s.

C. C. O'Brien (ed.), *The Shaping of Modern Ireland* (London, 1960).

R. F. Foster, *Modern Ireland, 1600–1972* (London, 1988).

CULTURE AND THE ARTS

W. W. Robson, *Modern English Literature* (Oxford, 1970), the best brief account.

B. Ford (ed.), *The Pelican Guide to English Literature*, vol. 7, *From James to Eliot* (rev. edn. London, 1983).

—— *The Pelican Guide to English Literature*, vol. 8, *The Present* (London, 1983).

B. Bergonzi (ed.), *The Twentieth Century: Sphere History of Literature in the English Language*, vol. 7 (London 1970).

John Gross, *Rise and Fall of the English Man of Letters* (London, 1969), a brilliant study.

Thomas Parry, *Hanes Llenyddiaeth Gymraeg hyd 1900* (Cardiff, 1944); English trans. H. I. Bell (Oxford, 1955), the standard survey of Welsh literature.

Percy Young, *A History of British Music* (London, 1967), the best work of its kind.

P. Kidson, P. Murray, and P. Thompson (eds.), *A History of English Architecture* (London, 1979).

Dennis Farr, *English Art, 1870–1940* (Oxford, 1978), including architecture.

Boris Ford (ed.), *The Cambridge Guide to the Arts in Britain*, vol. 8 (Cambridge, 1989), comprehensive.

Robert Hewinson, *In Anger: Culture and the Cold War* (London, 1981), an intelligent analysis.

——, *Too Much: Art and Society in the Sixties, 1960–75* (London, 1988).

CHRONOLOGY

VOL. I. ROMAN AND ANGLO-SAXON BRITAIN

55–54 BC	Expeditions of Caesar
49 BC	*Caesar defeats Pompey: effective end of Roman Republic**
	Julio-Claudian Emperors (27 BC–AD 68
34–26 BC	Projected expeditions of Augustus
	Britain between the invasions: period of political and economic change
by 12 BC	*Permanent Roman bases on Rhine*
AD 40	Expedition of Gaius cancelled
	Claudius (41–54)
by 43	Death of Cunobelinus
43	Claudian invasion
by 47	Conquest of south and east of England completed
49	Foundation of Colchester
c.50	Foundation of London
51	Defeat and capture of Caratacus
	Nero (54–68)
61	Revolt of Boudica
68–9	*'Year of the Four Emperors'*
	Flavian Emperors (69–96)
70–84	Conquest of Wales and north completed
	Conquest of Scotland
	Trajan (98–117)
c.100	Scotland temporarily lost: frontier on Tyne–Solway line *Hadrian (117–38)*
122	Hadrian in Britain: the Wall begun
	Antonine Emperors (138–92)
	Antoninus Pius (138–61)
140–3	Antonine advance into Scotland: by 143 Antonine Wall begun
c.158	Serious trouble in the north
? c.160	Temporary reoccupation of Antonine Wall

* Entries in *italics* denote events belonging to the history of the Roman Empire.

	Marcus Aurelius (161–80); major wars on the Danube
? c.163	Hadrian's Wall restored
193	Clodius Albinus proclaimed in Britain
	Severan Emperors (193–235)
196–213	Britain becomes two provinces
208–11	Campaigns of Septimius Severus and Caracalla in Scotland
235–70	*Imperial crisis: civil wars and invasions in East and West*
260–73	'Gallic Empire'
270s	Renewed growth in Britain
	Diocletian (284–305)
	'The Tetarchy'
287–96	Carausius and Allectus
296	Britain recovered by Constantius
after 296	Britain becomes a civil diocese of four provinces
	House of Constantius (305–63)
306	Campaign of Constantius I in Scotland; Constantine the Great proclaimed at York
324	*Constantine sole emperor; foundation of Constantinople*
340–69	Period of severe stress: internal troubles, harassment by barbarians
350	*Magnentius proclaimed in Gaul*
353	*Constantius II sole emperor*
353	Purge by Paul the Chain
	House of Valentinian (364–92)
367–9	'Barbarian Conspiracy', recovery and restoration of Britain by the elder Theodosius
	House of Theodosius (379–455)
	Theodosius the Great (379–95)
383	Magnus Maximus proclaimed in Britain; victory over Picts
	Honorius (395–423)
398–400	Victories over Picts, Scots, Saxons
400–2	Possible troop withdrawals by Stilicho
402/3	*Western imperial court withdrawn from Milan to Ravenna*
406	Britain revolts from Honorius: two emperors proclaimed

407	Constantine III proclaimed in Britain
	Constantine III rules from Arles (407–11)
409	Britain revolts from Constantine III: end of Roman rule in Britain
410	'Rescript of Honorius': letter to Britons (?), significance disputed
429	St. Germanus visits Britain
*c.*450	The *adventus Saxonum*: Hengest and Horsa settle in Kent (traditional date)
455	Hengest rebels against Vortigern (traditional date)
477	Saxon settlement of Sussex (traditional date)
495	Saxon settlement of Wessex (traditional date)
*c.*500	Battle of *Mons Badonicus*
560	Æthelberht, later over-king, becomes king in Kent
577	The West Saxons capture Gloucester, Cirencester and Bath
597	St. Augustine's mission arrives in Kent
616	Raedwald of East Anglia, as over-king, makes Edwin king of Northumbria
*c.*624	Death of Raedwald, and his probable burial in the Sutton Hoo barrow
627	Conversion of Edwin and the Northumbrian court
633	Battle of Heavenfield; Oswald of Northumbria becomes over-king
635	Conversion of King Cynegils of Wessex
642	Oswald is killed at Oswestry by King Penda of Mercia
655	Penda is defeated and killed at the *Winwaed* by Oswy of Northumbria, who becomes over-king
664	Synod of Whitby
669	Arrival of Archbishop Theodore
672	Synod of Hertford; battle of the Trent, marking the beginnings of the rise of Mercia
685–8	Expansion of Wessex under Caedwalla to include Kent, Surrey and Sussex
716	Æthelbald become king of Mercia
731	Bede completes his *Ecclesiastical History*
746–7	First Council of Clofesho
757	Death of Æthelbald; Offa becomes king of Mercia
786	Legatine Council held under Offa

793–5	Danish raids on Lindisfarne, Jarrow, and Iona
796	Death of Offa
825	Egbert of Wessex defeats Mercia and annexes Kent, Essex, Surrey, and Sussex
835	Big Danish raid on Kent
865	The Danish 'Great Army' lands
867	Northumbria falls to the Danes
870	East Anglia falls to the Danes; murder of St. Edmund
871	The Danes attack Wessex; Alfred becomes king
874	Mercia falls to the Danes
878	(March) The Danes drive Alfred into the Somerset marshes
	(May) Alfred defeats the Danes at Edington; Guthrum is baptized
899	Death of Alfred; Edward 'the Elder' becomes king of Wessex
910–20	Edward and Æthelflaed reconquer most of the Danelaw
919	Norse kingdom of York is founded by Raegnald
924	Death of Edward; Athelstan becomes king
937	Athelstan defeats the Norse, Scots and Strathclyde Welsh at Brunanburh
939	Death of Athelstan; Edmund become king
940	Dunstan begin to refound Glastonbury as a regular monastic house
946	Death of Edmund
954	The last king of York is deposed
959	Edgar becomes king
960	Dunstan becomes Archbishop of Canterbury
c.970	*Regularis Concordia* is compiled
973	Edgar is crowned and consecrated, and receives the submission of British princes
975	Death of Edgar; Edward 'the Martyr' becomes king
979	Murder of Edward; Æthelred 'the Unready' becomes king
991	The Danes defeat Alderman Byrhtnoth and the Essex levies at Maldon; treaty between England and Normandy
1002	Æthelred orders the massacre of all Danes in England

1003	Danish invasion led by King Swein
1013	Swein returns with a new army; the Danelaw accepts him as king
1014	Swein dies; the Danish army in England elect Cnut as their king
1016	(April) Æthelred dies; Edmund 'Ironside' becomes king
	(autumn) Cnut defeats Edmund at Ashingdon; Edmund dies and Cnut becomes King of all England
1017	Cnut divides England into four earldoms
1035	Death of Cnut
1037	Harold becomes king
1040	Death of Harold; Harthacnut becomes king
1042	Death of Harthacnut; Edward 'the Confessor' becomes king
1051–2	Conflict between King Edward and Godwin earl of Wessex
1053	Death of Godwin; his son Harold becomes earl of Wessex
1064–5	Earl Harold visits Duke William in Normandy
1066	(January) Death of King Edward; Earl Harold becomes king
	(September) King Harold of England defeats and kills King Harold of Norway at Stamford Bridge
	(October) Duke William of Normandy defeats and kills King Harold of England at Hastings

VOL. 2 THE MIDDLE AGES

1066	(December) William is consecrated king
1067–70	English rebellions
1069–70	The harrying of the north
1086	Domesday Survey carried out
1087	Death of William I; accession of William II Rufus
1088	Rebellion in support of Robert Curthose
1093	Anselm appointed Archbishop of Canterbury
1096	Robert pawns Normandy ot Rufus
1100	Death of William Rufus; accession of Henry I
1101	Invasion of Robert Curthose
1106	Battle of Tinchebray; Curthose imprisoned; Henry I takes Normandy
1107	Settlement of Investiture Dispute in England

1120	Wreck of the White Ship
1128	Marriage of Empress Matilda to Geoffrey of Anjou
1135	Death of Henry I; accession of Stephen
1139–53	Civil war in England
1141	Battle of Lincoln; Stephen captured; later exchanged for Robert of Gloucester
1141–5	Geoffrey of Anjou conquers Normandy
1149	Cession of Northumbria to David of Scotland
1152	Henry of Anjou (later Henry II) marries Eleanor of Aquitaine
1153	Henry invades England; he and Stephen come to terms
1154	Death of Stephen; accession of Henry II
1157	Henry regains Northumbria
1162	Becket appointed Archbishop of Canterbury
1164	Council and Constitutions of Clarendon; Becket goes into exile
1166	Assize of Clarendon
1169–72	English conquest of Ireland begins
1170	Coronation of the young king; murder of Becket
1173–4	Rebellion against Henry II; William 'the Lion' (king of Scotland) invades the north
1183	Death of the young king
1189	Death of Henry II; accession of Richard I
1190–92	Richard I on crusade
1193–4	Richard in prison in Germany
1193–1205	Hubert Walter, Archbishop of Canterbury (justiciar 1194–8; chancellor 1199–1205)
1197	Death of Rhys of Deheubarth
1199	Death of Richard I; accession of John; establishment of Chancery Rolls
1203–4	Philip Augustus conquers Anjou and Normandy
1208–14	Interdict in England
1214	Battle of Bouvines: French victory
1215	Magna Carta; civil war in England
1216	Louis (later Louis VIII) invades; death of John; accession of Henry III
1217	Battles of Lincoln and Dover; Louis withdraws
1221–4	Arrival of Dominican and Franciscan Friars in England
1224	Louis VIII completes conquest of Poitou

1232	Dismissal of Hubert de Burgh
1240	Death of Llywelyn the Great
1254	Henry III accepts papal offer of throne of Sicily
1258	Barons take over royal government; provisions of Oxford
1259	Treaty of Paris between England and France
1264	Battle of Lewes; Henry III captured; government of Simon de Montfort
1265	Battle of Evesham; killing of Simon de Montfort
1267	Henry recognizes Llywelyn ap Gruffydd as Prince of Wales
1272	Death of Henry III; accession of Edward I
1276–7	First Welsh War
1282–3	Edward's conquest of Wales
1286–9	Edward I in Gascony
1291	Edward I asserts his overlordship over Scotland
1294	War with France begins
1295	Franco-Scottish alliance
1296	Edward I invades Scotland; his conflict with the Church
1297	Edward I's conflict with his magnates; his expedition to Flanders
1306	Rebellion of Robert Bruce
1307	Death of Edward I; accession of Edward II
1314	Scottish victory at Bannockburn
1315–16	Great famine
1321–2	Civil war in England
1327	Deposition and death of Edward II; accession of Edward III
1330	Edward III takes the reins of government
1337	The Hundred Years War begins
1339–41	Political crisis in England
1346	English victories at Crécy and Neville's Cross
1347	English capture Calais
1348	First occurrence of plague in England
1356	English victory at Poitiers
1361	Second major occurrence of plague
1376	'Good Parliament' meets; death of Edward, the Black Prince
1377	Death of Edward III; accession of Richard II

1381	The Peasants' Revolt
1382	Condemnation of John Wycliffe's works
1388	'Merciless Parliament' meets; battle of Otterburn against the Scots
1389	Richard II declares himself of age
1394–5	Richard II's expedition to Ireland
1396	Anglo-French treaty
1397–9	Richard II's 'tyranny'
1399	Deposition of Richard II; accession of Henry IV
1400	Rebellion of Owain Glyndŵr begins (to 1410)
1403	Henry Hotspur defeated at Shrewsbury
1405	Execution of Archbishop Scrope of York
1408	Defeat of the earl of Northumberland at Bramham Moor
1413	Death of Henry IV; accession of Henry V
1415	English victory at Agincourt
1419–20	English conquest of Normandy
1420	Anglo-French treaty of Troyes
1422	Death of Henry V; accession of Henry VI
1435	Death of John, duke of Bedford; Franco-Burgundian treaty of Arras
1436–7	Henry VI comes of age
1445	Henry VI marries Margaret of Anjou
1449–50	French overrun Normandy
1450	Murder of the duke of Suffolk; John Cade's rebellion
1453	French overrun Gascony; Henry VI becomes ill
1455	Battle of St. Albans between Richard, duke of York and the royalist forces
1459	Defeat of the duke of York at Blore Heath and Ludford Bridge
1461	Deposition of Henry VI; accession of Edward IV
1465	Capture of Henry VI
1469	Rebellion of Richard, earl of Warwick and George, duke of Clarence
1470	Deposition of Edward IV; return of Henry VI
1471	Return of Edward IV; death of the earl of Warwick at Barnet; death of Henry VI
1475	Edward IV's expedition to France; Anglo-French treaty of Picquigny

1477	William Caxton's first printed book in England
1483	Death of Edward IV; accession, deposition, and death of Edward V; accession of Richard III; rebellion of Henry, duke of Buckingham
1485	Death of Richard III at Bosworth; accession of Henry VII

VOL. 3 THE TUDORS AND STUARTS

1487	Rebellion of Lambert Simnel
1491	Birth of Prince Henry
1509	Accession of Henry VIII
1510	Execution of Empson and Dudley
1512	War with France and Scotland
1513	Battle of Flodden: English victory over Scotland
1515	Wolsey appointed Lord Chancellor
1522	War with France
1525	Peace with France
1527	Divorce crisis begins
1528	War with Spain
1529	Peace of Cambrai; fall of Wolsey: Sir Thomas More succeeds as Lord Chancellor
1532	More resigns
1533	Henry VIII marries Anne Boleyn; Act of Appeals; birth of Princess Elizabeth
1534	Act of Supremacy
1535	Execution of More and Fisher
1536	Dissolution of the Monasteries; Pilgrimage of Grace; union of England and Wales
1542	Battle of Solway Moss; English victory over invading Scottish army
1543	War with France
1547	Succession of Edward VI; ascendancy of Protector Somerset; battle of Pinkie: English victory over Scotland
1549	First Book of Common Prayer; Northumberland's coup
1553	Accession of Mary
1554	Pole returns; reunion with Rome; Wyatt's rebellion
1555	Persecution of Protestants begins
1557	War with France

1558	New Book of Rates; accession of Elizabeth I
1559	Peace of Cateau-Cambrésis; religious Settlement in England
1566	Archbishop Parker's *Advertisements* demand religious conformity
1568	Mary Stuart flees to England
1569	Northern Rebellion
1570	Papal bull declares Elizabeth excommunicated and deposed
1580	Jesuit missionaries arrive in England
1585	War with Spain
1587	Execution of Mary Stuart
1588	Defeat of the Spanish Armada
1594	Bad harvests begin
1601	Essex's rebellion
1603	Death of Elizabeth; accession of James VI of Scotland as James I; peace in Ireland; Millenary Petition of the Puritans
1604	Peace with Spain (treaty of London); Hampton Court Conference (king, bishops, Puritans)
1605	Gunpowder Plot, the last major Catholic conspiracy
1606–7	Failure of James's plans for union of kingdoms
1607	Settlement of Virginia
1609	Rebellion of the Northern Earls in Ireland; beginnings of the Planting of Ulster by Scots and English Protestants
1610	Failure of Great Contract (reform of royal finance)
1611	Publication of Authorized Version of the Bible (Anglican–Puritan co-operation)
1612	Death of Prince Henry, James's promising elder son
1613	Marriage of Princess Elizabeth to Elector Palatine, Protestant zealot, enmeshed Britain in continental politics
1617–29	Ascendancy of George Villiers, duke of Buckingham
1919–22	Inigo Jones designs the Banqueting House, the first major royal public building since the reign of Henry VIII
1620	Pilgrim Fathers inaugurate religious migration to New England

1622–3	Prince Charles and Buckingham go to Spain to woo the king's daughter and are rebuffed
1624–30	War with Spain
1625	Death of James I; accession of Charles I and marriage to Henrietta Maria, sister of Louis XIII of France
1626–9	War with France
1628	Petition of Right; publication of Harvey's work on the circulation of the blood; assassination of Buckingham
1629	Charles I dissolves Parliament, determines to govern without one
1630	Large-scale emigration to Massachusetts begins
1633	William Laud translated to be Archbishop of Canterbury
1634–40	Ship Money case
1637	Hampden's case supports Charles I's claim to collect Ship Money
1637–40	Breakdown of Charles's government of Scotland and two attempts to impose his will by force
1640	Long Parliament summoned
1641	Remodelling of government in England and Scotland; abolition of conciliar courts, abolition of prerogative taxation, triennial bill, Grand Remonstrance; rebellion of Ulster Catholics
1642	King's attempt on the Five Members; his withdrawal from London; the 19 Propositions; the resort of arms: Civil War
1643	King's armies prosper; Scots invade on side of Parliament
1644	Parliamentary armies prosper, especially in the decisive battle of the war, Marston Moor (June)
1645	'Clubmen' risings of armed neutrals threaten both sides; Royalist armies disintegrate, but parliamentary forces reorganized (New Model Army)
1646	King surrenders to the Scots; bishops and Book of Common Prayer abolished, Presbyterian Church established
1647	Army revolt; radical movements criticize parliamentary tyranny; king prevaricates

1648	Second Civil War: Scots now side with the king and are defeated; provincial risings (Kent, Colchester, South Wales, Yorks., etc.) crushed
1649	Trial and execution of Charles I: England a Republic
1649–53	Government by sovereign single-chamber assembly, the 'Rump' Parliament thoroughly purged of royalists and moderates
1649–50	Oliver Cromwell conquers Ireland (Drogheda massacre)
1650–2	Oliver Cromwell conquers Scotland (battles of Dunbar and Worcester)
1651	Thomas Hobbes's *Leviathan* published
1652–4	First Dutch War
1653	Cromwell dissolves Rump, creates the Nominated or Barebones Assembly; it surrenders power back to him, and he becomes Lord Protector under a paper constitution (*The Instrument of Government*)
1655–60	War with Spain
1655	Royalist insurrection (Penruddock's rising) is a complete failure
1657	*Instrument of Government* replaced by a parliamentary paper constitution, the *Humble Petition and Advice*; Cromwell rejects title of King and remains Lord Protector, but nominates his own House of Lords
1658	Cromwell dies and is succeeded by his son Richard
1659	Richard overthrown by the army; Rump restored but displeases many in the army
1660	Charles II restored
1662	Church of England restored; Royal Society receives its Charter
1663	Failure of first royal attempt to grant religious toleration
1665–7	Second Dutch War
1665	Great Plague (final major outbreak)
1666	Great Fire of London
1667	Milton's *Paradise Lost* published
1672–3	Failure of second royal attempt to grant religious toleration
1672–4	Third Dutch War

1674   Grain bounties introduced (England self-sufficient in food)

1678   Titus Oates and the Popish Plot; Bunyan's *Pilgrim's Progress*, part I, published

1679–81   The Exclusion Crisis; emergence of Whig and Tory parties

1683   The Rye House Plot; Whigs proscribed

1685   Charles II dies; accession of James II; rebellion by Charles II's protestant bastard, the duke of Monmouth, fails

1687   James II's Declaration of Indulgence; Tories proscribed; Newton's *Principia Mathematica* published

1688   James II's son born

1688   William of Orange invades: James II takes flight, accession of William III (of Orange) and Mary

VOL. 4 THE EIGHTEENTH CENTURY AND THE AGE OF INDUSTRY

1689   Bill of Rights settles succession to the throne and declares illegal various grievances; Toleration Act grants rights to Trinitarian Protestant dissenters

1690   Battle of the Boyne: William III defeats Irish and French army

1694   Bank of England founded; death of Queen Mary; Triennial Act sets the maximum duration of a parliament at three years

1695   Lapse of Licensing Act

1697   Peace treaty of Ryswick between allied powers of the League of Augsburg and France; Civil List Act votes funds for the maintenance of the royal household

1701   War of Spanish Succession begins; Act of Settlement settles the royal succession on the descendants of Sophia of Hanover

1702   Death of William III; accession of Anne

1704   Battle of Blenheim: British, Dutch, German and Austrian troops defeat French and Bavarian forces; British capture of Gibraltar from Spain

1707   Union of England and Scotland

1710   Impeachment of Dr Sacheverell; Harley ministry

1713   Peace treaty of Utrecht concludes the War of Spanish Succession

1714	Death of Anne; accession of George I
1715	Jacobite rebellion aimed at overthrowing the Hanoverian succession fails
1716	Septennial Act sets the maximum duration of a parliament at seven years
1717	Whig split; suspension of convocation
1720	South Sea Bubble: many investors ruined after speculation in the stock of the South Sea Company
1721	Walpole ministry
1722	Atterbury Plot, the most notable Jacobite plot
1726	Jonathan Swift's *Gulliver's Travels* published
1727	Death of George I; accession of George II
1729	Alexander Pope's *Dunciad* published
1730	Walpole/Townshend split
1733	Excise crisis: Walpole has to abandon his plans to reorganize the customs and excise
1737	Death of Queen Caroline
1738	Wesley's 'conversion': the start of Methodism
1739	War of Jenkins' Ear: Anglo-Spanish naval war
1740	War of the Austrian Succession
1741	Samuel Richardson's *Pamela* published
1742	Fall of Walpole
1744	Ministry of Pelham
1745	Jacobite Rebellion led by 'Bonnie Prince Charlie'
1746	Battle of Culloden: the duke of Cumberland routs the Jacobite army
1748	Peace of Aix-la-Chapelle concludes War of the Austrian Succession
1752	Adoption of Gregorian Calendar
1753	Jewish Naturalization Bill
1754	Newcastle ministry
1756	Seven Years War: Britain allied with Frederick the Great of Prussian against France, Austria, and Russia
1757	Pitt–Newcastle ministry; battle of Plassey: British victory over Bengal
1759	Capture of Quebec: British victory over the French
1760	Death of George II; accession of George III
1761	Laurence Sterne's *Tristram Shandy* published
1762	Bute's ministry
1763	Peace of Paris concludes Seven Years War; Grenville

	ministry; Wilkes and General Warrants
1765	Rockingham ministry; American Stamp Act attempts to make the defence of the American colonies self-financing: repealed 1766
1766	Chatham ministry
1768	Grafton ministry; Middlesex election crisis
1769	James Watt's steam engine patented
1770	Lord North's ministry; Edmund Burke's *Thoughts on the Present Discontents* published; Falkland Islands crisis
1773	Boston Tea Party: American colonists protest against the East India Company's monopoly of tea exports to America
1774	Coercive Acts passed in retaliation for Boston Tea Party
1776	Declaration of American Independence; Edward Gibbon's *Decline and Fall* and Adam Smith's *Wealth of Nations* published
1779	Wyvill's Association movement
1780	Gordon Riots develop from a procession to petition parliament against the Catholic Relief Act
1781	Surrender at Yorktown: American victory over British troops
1782	Second Rockingham ministry
1783	Shelburne ministry; Peace of Versailles recognizes independence of American colonies; Fox–North coalition; Younger Pitt's ministry
1784	East India Act
1785	Pitt's motion for parliamentary reform defeated
1786	Eden commercial treaty with France
1789	French Revolution
1790	Edmund Burke's *Reflections on the Revolution in France* published
1791	Thomas Paine's *The Rights of Man* published
1792	Coal gas used for lighting; Mary Wollstonecraft's *Vindication of the Rights of Women* published
1793	Outbreak of war with France; voluntary Board of Agriculture set up; commercial depression
1795	'Speenhamland' system of outdoor relief adopted, making up wages to equal cost of subsistence

1796	Vaccination against smallpox introduced
1798	T. R. Malthus's *Essay on Population* published; tax of ten per cent on incomes over £200 introduced
1799	Trade Unions suppressed; Napoleon appointed First Consul in France
1799–1801	Commercial boom
1801	Union with Ireland; first British Census
1802	Peace with France; Peel introduces first factory legislation
1803	War with France; General Enclosure Act simplifies process of enclosure of common land
1805	Battle of Trafalgar: Nelson defeats the French and Spanish fleets
1809–10	Commercial boom
1811	Depression because of Orders in Council; 'Luddite' disturbances in Nottinghamshire and Yorkshire; George, Prince of Wales, made Prince Regent
1813	East India Company's monopoly abolished
1815	Battle of Waterloo: defeat of Napoleon; peace in Europe: Congress of Vienna; Corn Law passed setting price of corn at 80s. per quarter
1815–17	Commercial boom
1817	Slump; the Blanketeers' march and other disturbances
1819	Peterloo massacre: troops intervene at mass reform meeting, killing 11 and wounding 400
1820	Death of George III; accession of George IV
1821–3	Famine in Ireland
1824	Commercial boom
1825	Trade Unions legalized; Stockton and Darlington railway opens; commercial depression
1829	Catholic Emancipation, ending most denials or restrictions of Catholic civil rights, ownership of property, and holding of public office
1830	Death of George IV; accession of William IV; Liverpool and Manchester railway opens
1830–2	First major cholera epidemic; Whigs in power under Grey
1831	'Swing' riots in rural areas against the mechanization of agriculture
1832	Great Reform Bill brings climax to period of political

reform, enlarging the franchise and restructuring representation in Parliament

1833   Factory Act limits child labour; beginning of Oxford Movement in Anglican Church

1834   Slavery abolished in the British Empire; parish workhouses instituted; Robert Owen founds the Grand National Consolidated Trade Union: action by government against 'illegal oaths' in unionism results in failure of GNCTU and transportation of six 'Tolpuddle Martyrs'

1835   Municipal Reform Act extends local government franchise to all ratepayers

1835–6   Commercial boom: 'little' railway mania

1837   Death of William IV; accession of Queen Victoria

1838   Anti-Corn Law League established; People's Charter drafted

1839   Chartist riots

1840   Penny post instituted

1841   Tories in power: Peel ministry

1844   Bank Charter Act; Rochdale Co-operative Society founded; Royal Commission on Health of Towns

1844–5   Railway mania: massive speculation and investment leads to building of 5,000 miles of track; potato famine begins in Ireland

1846   Corn Law abolished; Whigs in power

1848   Revolutions in Europe; Public Health Act

VOL. 5 THE MODERN AGE

1851   Great Exhibition

1852   Derby's first minority Conservative government

1852–5   Aberdeen's coalition government

1853   Gladstone's first budget

1854   Northcote–Trevelyan civil service report

1854–6   Crimean War, defending European interests in the Middle East against Russia

1855   Palmerston's first government

1857–8   Second Opium War opens China to European trade

1858–9   Derby's second minority Conservative government

1858   Indian Mutiny and India Act

1859   Publication of Darwin's *Origin of Species*

1859–65	Palmerston's second Liberal government
1860	Anglo-French 'Cobden' treaty and Gladstone's budget codify and extend principles of free trade
1861	Death of Albert, Prince Consort
1862	Limited Liability Act provides vital stimulus to accumulation of capital in shares
1865	Death of Palmerston (October)
1865–6	Russell's second Liberal government
1866	Russell–Gladstone moderate Reform Bill fails
1866–8	Derby's third minority Conservative government
1867	Derby–Disraeli Reform Act; Dominion of Canada Act
1868	Disraeli succeeds Derby as Prime Minister (February)
1868–74	Gladstone's first Liberal government
1869	Suez Canal opened; Irish Church disestablished
1870	Irish Land Act; Forster–Ripon English Elementary Education Act; Married Women's Property Act extends the rights of women in marriage
1872	Scottish Education Act
1873	Gladstone government resigns after defeat on Irish Universities Bill; Disraeli declines to take office
1874–80	Disraeli's second Conservative government
1875	Disraeli buys Suez Canal shares, gaining a controlling interest for Britain
1875	Agricultural depression deepens
1875–6	R. A. Cross's Conservative social reforms passed
1876	Victoria proclaimed Empress of India; massacres of Christians in Turkish Bulgaria provoke anti-Turkish campaign in Britain, led by Gladstone
1877	Confederation of British and Boer states in South Africa
1878	Congress of Berlin; Disraeli announces 'peace with honour'
1879	Trade depression; Zulu War: British defeated at Isandhlwana, win at Ulundi
1879–80	Gladstone's Midlothian campaign denounces imperialism in Afghanistan and South Africa
1880–5	Gladstone's second Liberal government
1880–1	First Anglo-Boer War
1881	Irish Land and Coercion Acts

1882	Britain occupies Egypt; Triple Alliance between Germany, Austria, and Italy
1884–5	Reform and Redistribution Acts
1885	Death of Gordon at Khartoum; Burma annexed; Salisbury's first (minority) Conservative government
1886	Royal Niger Company chartered; gold found in Transvaal; Gladstone's third Liberal government introduces first Home Rule Bill for Ireland: Liberal Party splits
1886–92	Salisbury's second (Conservative–Liberal-Unionist) government
1887	British East Africa Company chartered
1888	County Councils Act establishes representative county authorities
1889	London dock strike; British South Africa Company chartered
1892–4	Gladstone's fourth (minority) Liberal government
1893	Second Home Rule Bill rejected by the Lords; Independent Labour Party founded
1894–5	Rosebery's minority Liberal government
1895–1902	Salisbury's third Unionist ministry
1896–8	Sudan conquered
1898	German naval expansion begins
1899–1902	Second Anglo-Boer War
1899	(autumn)British disasters in South Africa
1900	Khaki election won by Salisbury; formation of Labour Representation Committee; Commonwealth of Australia Act
1901	Death of Victoria; accession of Edward VII
1902	Balfour's Education Act; Anglo-Japanese alliance
1902–5	Balfour's Unionist government
1903	Chamberlain's Tariff Reform campaign starts
1904	Anglo-French *Entente*
1905–8	Campbell-Bannerman's Liberal government
1906	Liberals win general election (January); Labour Party formed
1907	Anglo-Russian *Entente*
1908–15	Asquith's Liberal government
1908	Asquith's Old Age Pensions plan introduced

1909	Churchill's Employment Exchanges introduced; Lloyd George's budget rejected by Lords; Union of South Africa Act
1910	(January) General election: Liberal government retains office
	(May) Death of Edward VII; accession of George V
	(December) General election: Liberal government again retains office
1911	Parliament Act curtails power of the House of Lords, establishes five-yearly elections; Lloyd George's National Insurance Act; Moroccan crisis
1911–12	Railway, mining, and coal strikes
1912	Anglo-German navy talks fail
1912–14	Third Home Rule Act (for Ireland) and Welsh Church Disestablishment Act passed, but suspended
1914	(28 June) Assassination of Archduke Ferdinand at Sarajevo
	(4 August) British Empire enters the First World War
1915–16	Dardanelles expedition, ending in British withdrawal from Gallipoli
1916	Battle of the Somme; battle of Jutland; Lloyd George succeeds Asquith as Prime Minister
1917	Battle of Passchendaele
1918	End of First World War (11 November); Lloyd George coalition government returned in 'coupon election' (December)
1919	Treaty of Versailles establishes peace in Europe
1921	Miners seek support of dockers' and railwaymen's unions (the 'Triple Alliance') in major strike: on 'Black Friday' the dockers and railwaymen back down, and the alliance is broken; Lloyd George concludes treaty with Sinn Fein
1922	Fall of Lloyd George; Bonar Law heads Conservative government
1923	Baldwin becomes Conservative Prime Minister; general election
1924	(January) MacDonald leads first Labour government
	(November) Conservatives return to office under Baldwin

1925	Britain goes back on the gold standard
1926	General Strike (3–12 May)
1929	General election; MacDonald leads second Labour government
1931	Financial crisis and run on the pound; Britain abandons the gold standard; MacDonald resigns and is returned in the election to head National government
1932	Ottawa Conference on imperial trade institutes protective tarriffs
1935	Conservatives win general election: Baldwin succeeds MacDonald as Prime Minister; Hoare–Laval pact on Abyssinia; Government of India Act
1936	Death of King George V; abdication of Edward VIII: George VI becomes king
1937	Neville Chamberlain succeeds Baldwin as Conservative Prime Minister
1938	Chamberlain meets Hitler at Berchtesgaden, Godesberg, and Munich
1939	British guarantee to Poland; British Empire declares war on Germany (3 September)
1940	Churchill succeeds Chamberlain as Prime Minister; withdrawal from Dunkirk; Battle of Britain
1941	*Luftwaffe* 'blitz' on many British cities; Soviet Union and United States enter the war
1942	Loss of Singapore; Montgomery's victory at El Alamein; battle of Stalingrad; Beveridge Report on social security
1943	Successful campaign in North Africa; Anglo-American armies invade Italy
1944	D-day invasion of France; Butler's Education Act
1945	End of war in Europe (8 May) and in far East (15 August); general election: massive Labour victory and Attlee becomes Prime Minister
1947	Coal and other industries nationalized; convertibility crisis; transfer of power to independent India, Pakistan, and Burma
1949	NATO founded; devaluation of the pound by Cripps
1950	General election: Labour retains power by narrow

	majority; outbreak of war in Korea
1951	Festival of Britain; general election: Conservatives defeat Labour, and Churchill again becomes Prime Minister
1952	Death of King George VI; Queen Elizabeth II proclaimed
1954	British troops withdraw from Egypt
1955	Eden becomes Prime Minister; general election won by Conservatives
1956	Anglo-French invasion of Suez, followed by withdrawal
1957	Eden resigns; Macmillan becomes Prime Minister
1959	General election: Conservatives win with larger majority
1963	French veto Britain's application to join the European Common Market; test-ban treaty in Moscow limits nuclear testing; Douglas-Home succeeds Macmillan as Prime Minister
1964	General election: Labour under Harold Wilson win narrow majority
1966	General election: Labour win with much larger majority
1967	Devaluation of the pound
1970	General election: Conservatives under Edward Heath returned to office
1972	National miners' strike; Stormont government abolished in Northern Ireland
1973	Britain enters European Common Market
1974	National miners' strike; two general elections: Labour under Harold Wilson win both with narrow majorities
1975	Popular referendum confirms British membership of the Common Market
1976	Economic crisis: Britain obtains help from International Monetary Fund
1979	Devolution referendums in Wales and Scotland; general election: Conservatives under Mrs Thatcher returned to office; independence granted to Zimbabwe (Rhodesia)
1980	Britain becomes self-sufficient in North Sea oil

1981	Social Democratic Party founded
1982	Britain defeats Argentina in war over the Falkland Islands
1983	General election: Mrs Thatcher's Conservative government returned with massive majority; Cruise missiles installed
1984	Miners' strike
1985	Miners' strike ends after a year; Anglo-Irish Hillsborough Agreement signed
1986	Channel Tunnel treaty signed; 'Big Bang' in Stock Exchange
1987	General election: Mrs Thatcher's Conservative government again returned with a majority of over 100; Stock Exchange collapse in the autumn
1989	Poll tax introduced
1990	Resignation of Mrs Thatcher; John Major becomes Prime Minister
1991	Gulf War against Iraq

DESCENDANTS OF QUEEN VICTORIA

PRIME MINISTERS 1851–1990

Lord John Russell	June 1846	Herbert Henry	
Earl of Derby	Feb. 1852	Asquith	Apr. 1908
Earl of Aberdeen	Dec. 1852	David Lloyd George	Dec. 1916
Viscount Palmerston	Feb. 1855	Andrew Bonar Law	Oct. 1922
Earl of Derby	Feb. 1858	Stanley Baldwin	May 1923
Viscount Palmerston	June 1859	James Ramsay	
Earl Russell	Oct. 1865	MacDonald	Jan. 1924
Earl of Derby	June 1866	Stanley Baldwin	Nov. 1924
Benjamin Disraeli	Feb. 1868	James Ramsay	
William Ewart		MacDonald	June 1929
Gladstone	Dec. 1868	Stanley Baldwin	June 1935
Benjamin Disraeli	Feb. 1874	Neville Chamberlain	May 1937
William Ewart		Winston Churchill	May 1940
Gladstone	Apr. 1880	Clement Attlee	July 1945
Marquess of Salisbury	June 1885	Winston Churchill	Oct. 1951
William Ewart		Sir Anthony Eden	Apr. 1955
Gladstone	Feb. 1886	Harold Macmillan	Jan. 1957
Marquess of Salisbury	July 1886	Sir Alec Douglas-	
William Ewart		Home	Oct. 1963
Gladstone	Aug. 1892	Harold Wilson	Oct. 1964
Earl of Rosebery	Mar. 1894	Edward Heath	June 1970
Marquess of Salisbury	June 1895	Harold Wilson	Mar. 1974
Arthur James Balfour	July 1902	James Callaghan	Apr. 1976
Sir Henry Campbell-		Margaret Thatcher	May 1979
Bannerman	Dec. 1905	John Major	Nov. 1990

FURTHER READING

1. THE LIBERAL AGE

GENERAL SURVEYS

Asa Briggs, *The Age of Improvement* (London, 1959), a good political and social survey of the period up to 1867.

D. Read, *England 1868–1914* (London, 1979), a competent, detailed survey.

Geoffrey Best, *Mid-Victorian Britain 1851–1870* (London, 1971), a predominantly social account.

R. C. K. Ensor, *England, 1870–1914* (Oxford, 1936, often reprinted), still has material and analysis of value.

E. Halévy, *History of the English People in the Nineteenth Century*, vols. 5 (*Imperialism and the Rise of Labour, 1895–1905*) and 6 (*The Rule of Democracy, 1905–1914*) (rev. edn. London, 1951–2), a classic account, based on contemporary published material, which still holds its own.

ECONOMIC HISTORY

P. Mathias, *The First Industrial Nation* (2nd rev. edn. London, 1983), a clear and concise account.

E. Hobsbawm, *Industry and Empire* (London, 1968), an incisive argument, stressing the socio-economic shift from industry to commerce.

D. Landes, *The Unbound Prometheus. Technological Change, 1750 to the Present* (Cambridge, 1969), the relationship of technology to industry.

SOCIAL LIFE

H. J. Dyos and M. Wolff (eds.), *The Victorian City*, 2 vols. (London, 1973), splendidly comprehensive illustrations.

G. Mingay (ed.), *The Victorian Countryside*, 2 vols. (London, 1981), the complementary work.

Robert Roberts, *The Classic Slum* (London, 1971), childhood in Salford.

OXFORD

MORE OXFORD PAPERBACKS

Details of a selection of other Oxford Paperbacks follow. A complete list of Oxford Paperbacks, including The World's Classics, Twentieth-Century Classics, OPUS, Past Masters, Oxford Authors, Oxford Shakespeare, and Oxford Paperback Reference, is available in the UK from the General Publicity Department, Oxford University Press (RS), Walton Street, Oxford, OX2 6DP.

In the USA, complete lists are available from the Paperbacks Marketing Manager, Oxford University Press, 200 Madison Avenue, New York, NY 10016.

Oxford Paperbacks are available from all good bookshops. In case of difficulty, customers in the UK can order direct from Oxford University Press Bookshop, 116 High Street, Oxford, Freepost, OX1 4BR, enclosing full payment. Please add 10 per cent of the published price for postage and packing.

HISTORY IN OXFORD PAPERBACKS

As the Oxford Paperbacks' history list grows, so does the range of periods it covers, from the Pharaohs to Anglo-Saxon England, and from Early Modern France to the Second World War.

EGYPT AFTER THE PHARAOHS

Alan K. Bowman

The thousand years between Alexander the Great's invasion in 332 BC and the Arab conquest in AD 642 was a period of enormous change and vitality in the history of Egypt. The Hellenistic era under the powerful Ptolemies ended with the defeat of Antony and Cleopatra in 30 BC, and Egypt became a province of Rome.

Throughout the millenium, however, many of the customs and belief of old Egypt survived, adapting themselves to the new rulers, who were in turn influenced by Egyptian culture. The heritage of the Egypt of the Pharaohs remained a vital force in the history of the land until the coming of Islam.

A vast collection of papyrus texts has survived from this period recording not only the great events but the everyday letters, lawsuits, accounts, and appeals of ordinary Egyptians. From these texts and from the evidence of archaeology, Dr Bowman draws together the Egyptian, Greek, and Roman strands of the story, presenting a masterly survey of the history, economy, and social life of Egypt in this thousand year span.

'eminently readable . . . should be studied by anyone who is seeking details of everyday life in the Roman period' *British Archaeological News*

Also in Oxford Paperbacks:

A History of the Vikings Gwyn Jones
A Turbulent, Seditious, and Factious People Christopher Hill
The Duel in European History V. G. Kiernan

HISTORY IN OXFORD PAPERBACKS

Oxford Paperbacks' superb history list offers books on a wide range of topics from ancient to modern times, whether general period studies or assessments of particular events, movements, or personalities.

THE STRUGGLE FOR
THE MASTERY OF EUROPE 1848–1918

A. J. P. Taylor

The fall of Metternich in the revolutions of 1848 heralded an era of unprecedented nationalism in Europe, culminating in the collapse of the Hapsburg, Romanov, and Hohenzollern dynasties at the end of the First World War. In the intervening seventy years the boundaries of Europe changed dramatically from those established at Vienna in 1815. Cavour championed the cause of *Risorgimento* in Italy; Bismarck's three wars brought about the unification of Germany; Serbia and Bulgaria gained their independence courtesy of the decline of Turkey—'the sick man of Europe'; while the great powers scrambled for places in the sun in Africa. However, with America's entry into the war and President Wilson's adherence to idealistic internationalist principles, Europe ceased to be the centre of the world, although its problems, still primarily revolving around nationalist aspirations, were to smash the Treaty of Versailles and plunge the world into war once more.

A. J. P. Taylor has drawn the material for his account of this turbulent period from the many volumes of diplomatic documents which have been published in the five major European languages. By using vivid language and forceful characterization, he has produced a book that is as much a work of literature as a contribution to scientific history.

'One of the glories of twentieth-century writing.' *Observer*

Also in Oxford Paperbacks:

Portrait of an Age: Victorian England   G. M. Young
Germany 1866–1945   Gorden A. Craig
The Russian Revolution 1917–1932   Sheila Fitzpatrick
France 1848–1945   Theodore Zeldin

OPUS

General Editors: Christopher Butler,
Robert Evans, Alan Ryan

OPUS is a series of accessible introductions to a wide range of studies in the sciences and humanities.

METROPOLIS

Emrys Jones

Past civilizations have always expressed themselves in great cities, immense in size, wealth, and in their contribution to human progress. We are still enthralled by ancient cities like Babylon, Rome, and Constantinople. Today, giant cities abound, but some are pre-eminent. As always, they represent the greatest achievements of different cultures. But increasingly, they have also been drawn into a world economic system as communications have improved.

Metropolis explores the idea of a class of supercities in the past and in the present, and in the western and developing worlds. It analyses the characteristics they share as well as those that make them unique; the effect of technology on their form and function; and the problems that come with size—congestion, poverty and inequality, squalor—that are sobering contrasts to the inherent glamour and attraction of great cities throughout time.

Also available in OPUS:

The Medieval Expansion of Europe J. R. S. Phillips
Metaphysics: The Logical Approach José A. Bernadete
The Voice of the Past 2/e Paul Thompson
Thinking About Peace and War Martin Ceadel

ART AND ARCHITECTURE IN
OXFORD PAPERBACKS

Oxford Paperbacks offers a growing list of art and architecture books, ranging from Michael Baxandall on Renaissance Italy to George Melly on pop art and from Anthony Blunt on art theory to Bram Dijkstra on fin-de-siècle 'erotic' art.

ENGLISH PARISH CHURCHES AS
WORKS OF ART
Alec Clifton-Taylor

In the course of his life Alec Clifton-Taylor visited thousands of churches and recorded his observations and opinions on their merits. The result, in this book, is not a dry analysis of the chronological evolution of churches and their styles, but a revealing tour of the parish church with the greatest emphasis on aesthetic value.

As all those who got to know him through his television appearances will agree, Alec Clifton-Taylor was the ideal guide to architecture—deeply knowledgeable and enthusiastic in his responses. His first book, *The Pattern of English Building*, is regarded as a classic and his popular BBC television series, *Six English Towns*, and its sequels, claimed a wide audience.

'"What a church!" writes Alec Clifton-Taylor of Walpole St Peter in Norfolk . . . "an unforgettable experience" . . . [Mr Clifton-Taylor] was one of the most individual, civilized, and lovable historians I have ever met.' Patrick Nuttgens, *Times Higher Educational Supplement*

Also in Oxford Paperbacks:

Painting and Experience in 15th-century Italy
Michael Baxandall
American Buildings and their Architects: The Colonial and Neo-Classical Styles   William H. Pierson
Vision and Design   Roger Fry
Revolt into Style   George Melly

PAST MASTERS

General Editor: Keith Thomas

Past Masters is a series of authoritative studies that introduce students and general readers alike to the thought of leading intellectual figures of the past whose ideas still influence many aspects of modern life.

'This Oxford University Press series continues on its encyclopaedic way ... One begins to wonder whether any intelligent person can afford not to possess the whole series.' *Expository Times*

KIERKEGAARD

Patrick Gardiner

Søren Kierkegaard (1813–55), one of the most original thinkers of the nineteenth century, wrote widely on religious, philosophical, and literary themes. But his idiosyncratic manner of presenting some of his leading ideas initially obscured their fundamental import.

This book shows how Kierkegaard developed his views in emphatic opposition to prevailing opinions, including certain metaphysical claims about the relation of thought to existence. It describes his reaction to the ethical and religious theories of Kant and Hegel, and it also contrasts his position with doctrines currently being advanced by men like Feuerbach and Marx. Kierkegaard's seminal diagnosis of the human condition, which emphasizes the significance of individual choice, has arguably been his most striking philosophical legacy, particularly for the growth of existentialism. Both that and his arresting but paradoxical conception of religious belief are critically discussed, Patrick Gardiner concluding this lucid introduction by indicating salient ways in which they have impinged on contemporary thought.

Also available in Past Masters:

Disraeli John Vincent
Freud Anthony Storr
Hume A. J. Ayer
Augustine Henry Chadwick